[Holy Communion]

Other Books in the Belief Matters Series

Incarnation by William H. Willimon

Belief Matters

[Holy Communion]

Celebrating God with Us

Kenneth M. Loyer

General Editor, William H. Willimon

Abingdon Press
Nashville

HOLY COMMUNION:
CELEBRATING GOD WITH US

Copyright © 2014 by Abingdon Press

This book is printed on acid-free paper.

Library of Congress Cataloging-in-Publication Data

Loyer, Kenneth.
Holy communion : celebrating God with us / by Kenneth M. Loyer.
    pages cm.—(Belief matters ; 2)
Includes bibliographical references.
ISBN 978-1-4267-9633-3 (binding: pbk. / trade : alk. paper)   1. Lord's Supper.   I. Title.
BV825.3.L69 2014
264'.36—dc23

2014019271

14 15 16 17 18 19 20 21 22 23—10 9 8 7 6 5 4 3 2 1
MANUFACTURED IN THE UNITED STATES OF AMERICA

In memory of Lois Turner Dees (1954–2013), whose life demonstrated the love and beauty of communion with God

Contents

Acknowledgments

Communion with God is not an exclusively individual endeavor, but is inherently communal. The same is true, at least to some extent, of writing a book. Numerous people have helped make this book possible. In particular, I thank Kathy Armistead of Abingdon Press for her belief in and support of this project; Will Willimon, General Editor of the Belief Matters series, for designing a book series that explores key Christian beliefs and for including my work in that series; and Shannon Vowell and John Stanley, whose valuable feedback helped shape the final product. I also acknowledge the people of my home church, St. Paul's United Methodist Church in Red Lion, Pennsylvania, where I was baptized and raised in the faith, learned to serve and follow Jesus Christ, and first received Communion. I give thanks for the many faithful Christians from that congregation who taught me about the importance of life with God. In addition, I express my gratitude to the people of Otterbein United Methodist Church of Spry in York, Pennsylvania. I have had the privilege of serving this wonderful congregation since 2010. It has been a joy for me to be their pastor and for us to experience together the new life that God has brought about in our midst. One of my primary reasons for writing this book is to share that story of renewal, and to do so in the firm belief that what God has done to revitalize that congregation, surely God can do elsewhere.

Finally, a special word of thanks goes to my wife, Molly, and our children, Annie and Zeke. From the time when I first shared the idea for this project up until its completion, Molly's steadfast encouragement and support have proven essential. I wrote much of this material shortly after two major life events, the passing of Molly's beloved mother, Lois Turner Dees, and the birth of our son. We named him Ezekiel, which means "God strengthens." One reason we chose that name was because our family had recently walked through what the psalmist calls "the valley of the shadow of death" (Psalm 23:4 NKJV) as Lois bravely battled the cancer that later took her life. Throughout that difficult journey, she showed unwavering faith and strength—the kind of faith and strength that bear powerful witness to the love of God, which is stronger than death, through the abiding presence of Jesus Christ, who is God with us. To Lois's blessed memory I dedicate this book.

Editor's Introduction

Belief Matters is a series that takes as its task the joyful celebration of the wonder of Christian believing. This task is accomplished by asking some of the best thinkers in the church to share with others, in a direct, accessible, pastoral way, why they enjoy thinking about Christian doctrine.

I know, I know, *doctrine* is a word that has a dry, dull sound to it. Stand up in your average church and announce, "And now we're going to talk about doctrine," and watch the eyelids droop and the congregation's thoughts wander elsewhere.

Belief Matters will change how you think about Christian thinking. I believe you'll find that Ken Loyer knows how to talk about doctrine in a way that keeps your joyful, prayerful attention from the first to the last. Here is doctrine not only as something you believe but also as something you do. Here is the Christian faith not only affirmed but also actively embodied, enacted, and performed in bread and wine on Sunday in church so that we may better perform the faith Monday through Saturday in the world.

In the dramatic reform of the Roman Catholic Church, Vatican II, as the Council at last turned its attention to sweeping reforms of the church's liturgy, Pope John XXIII urged the Council to be bold, to "open up the riches of the church's faith to the faithful." That's what Belief Matters aims to do and that's what Ken's book accomplishes for the Lord's Supper or Holy Communion. You will quickly find that Ken opens up a ritual that we perform in church into a sign that encompasses the whole of Christian life. In receiving Christ's body and blood in the ritual of Communion at church, we are acting our way into a new way of thinking. We are performing with our bodies that which we pray will take over our souls. And, by God's grace, it does. As Augustine said, in Communion God works a great miracle: "We become as we profess."

In my book *Incarnation,* the first book in the Belief Matters series, I tried to talk about the mysterious wonder of God as God With Us. In the incarnation of Jesus Christ, we find out the truth about God as Emmanuel. Ken's book is a perfect sequel to such a deep, life-changing thought as the doctrine of incarnation. Our God is constantly, relentlessly seeking Communion. Even as God—Father, Son, and Holy Spirit are in constant communication and Communion, so God in Christ offers to be in Communion with us.

As John Calvin, great reformer of the church, once said of Holy Communion, God never forgets that we are animals. So thank God that God does not deal with us as the angels we are not, but as the creatures we really are. God condescends to be God With Us before we attempt to be with God. God doesn't limit Communion with creation to sporadic, miraculous, spectacular displays of divine presence. God comes to us in something as ordinary and mundane, as essential and revealing as eating and drinking. In sharing bread and wine, in giving thanks to God for all God's daily good gifts, in joining with sisters and brothers in a meal, God is with us. God meets us where we are and responds to us as we are—creatures in daily need of God's loving gifts and God's near presence among us.

So, read *Holy Communion: Celebrating God with Us* in much the same way as your pastor bids you to celebrate the Eucharist on Sunday. After the wine is poured and the bread is blessed, in most churches the pastor calls forth, "The gifts of God for the people of God." Then the congregation answers with one voice, "Thanks be to God!"

—Will Willimon

"Are We Having Communion Today?"

When the hour came, [Jesus] took his place at the table, and the apostles with him. He said to them, "I have eagerly desired to eat this Passover with you before I suffer; for I tell you, I will not eat it until it is fulfilled in the kingdom of God."

—Luke 22:14-16

"Communion Sundays are my *favorite!*" exclaimed eight-year-old Hannah to her mother. A spiritually sensitive young girl, Hannah participates actively in the church I serve. Her enthusiasm for Communion derives in part from the fact that she loves the taste of Communion bread. On a deeper level, it is also the act of sharing in this holy meal together as a church family that she finds meaningful even at her young age.

One Sunday morning during the frantic rush to get ready for church, Hannah asked her mom, "Are we having Communion today?" She was asking, of course, whether Communion would be part of worship for us that morning in our church. She then told her mom, enthusiastically, that she really hoped it would be. Yet the question points beyond the original context to a deeper meaning: Are we, as the church—at the local level, at the denominational level, and in the wider church—truly having Communion today, in this day and in this age? In other words, are we communing with Christ as closely as he invites and commands us? In that sense, are we having Communion today?

We all seek communion, or fellowship of some sort, in the hope that it will bring us happiness and fulfillment. We all seek fulfillment somewhere, in something, whether it is positive or negative, healthy or not. Some people seek a kind of communion with their possessions, a common path in an age of rampant materialism. Others seek communion with themselves by relying on their own egos, reputation, or social status in the quest for ultimate satisfaction. Still, for others the way to try to make life complete is marked by professional success, hobbies, or another human being through friendship and love. Not all the places or people we turn to for fulfillment are bad. To be human is to seek communion with something or someone, to seek happiness and meaning, to know and be known, and to love and be loved. That is a natural desire, but we should ask ourselves what kind of communion we are seeking, and why.

In our quest for a good and meaningful life, where do we ultimately turn? At root, these are spiritual matters. Even among regular churchgoers, Holy Communion might be little more than an afterthought as a resource for the sustenance that we crave. Yet this sacred meal is a gift of God that directly addresses the hunger of the human heart. What makes Holy Communion holy—set apart, special, and of God—is the spiritual nourishment that it provides through the work of the Holy Spirit in our ongoing relationship with God.

The Lord's Supper, like baptism, gives our worship of God a vital objectivity that stands out in an otherwise too comfortably pious and experiential church. We cannot reduce the meaning of the Eucharist (another name for Holy Communion, based on the Greek word for "thanksgiving" or "gratitude") to a mere subjective, inner experience of God. Over against such minimalist approaches, in this sacrament the Word of God breaks through to us on God's own terms, not on ours, and it is above all God's action. Holy Communion is not first something that we do, but a divine doing that we undergo, by faith, as we receive these gifts of God that draw us more deeply into the mystery of our redemption through Christ. Here at the Lord's altar, almighty God does what needs doing—taking, blessing, breaking, and giving the sacrament of Christ's body and blood given for and to the world, so that, as Christ's people, we might also be taken, blessed, broken, and given for the world in his name.

There is a great need to recover a richer theology and practice of this sacrament in the church today because that is a key to strengthening our life in Christ. It is also, I believe, a way for us and our congregations to experience genuine renewal. In the past, proper celebration of the Eucharist has sown seeds of awakening and revitalization. Today we see signs of a growing interest among many Christians in reclaiming a deeper appreciation for Holy Communion.

Acting on that interest has been crucial to the renewal of the church I serve. It is a story that will be woven throughout the pages of this book with anecdotes and insights from what I have learned in pastoral ministry. Our church's journey of growth is not, in itself, exceptionally noteworthy or outstanding. Yet what God has done among us—reflected in part through an increase in average weekly attendance from under 90 in 2010 to over 170 in 2014—has given new hope to the people of Otterbein United Methodist Church of Spry in York, Pennsylvania, and has enabled us to do more to serve our community in Christ's name and to grow closer to God and each other as a church family. For those reasons as well as others, this is a story worth telling, and people from other congregations may be able to benefit from hearing it. I can confidently claim that the recent growth God has brought about in and through our church has been fueled by a renewed commitment to prayer and to regular participation in the Lord's Supper.

The institution of a midweek service of Holy Communion has played a large part in our turnaround, a far greater role indeed than what the average attendance of roughly a dozen people at midweek worship suggests. God has used that group to make prayer, Scripture, and Communion a more central focus for the congregation as a whole, and the results have been encouraging and exciting to see. In any setting, regardless of number or size, what matters most is for our hearts to be opened by grace to the God who can transform and renew us. As we abide in Christ by faith, God will bear spiritual fruit in our hearts and lives, in our churches, and in the world around us. It will be beautiful to behold.

The purpose of this book is to encourage us all to return to what John Wesley, the spiritual father of the Methodist movement, called one of the three chief means of grace or ways in which the presence of God becomes accessible to us: the Lord's Supper.[1] In what follows, I want to invite us all to respond in greater faith to the invitation of Christ himself for us to do as he commands, that is, to take, eat, and drink of the sacrament of his body and blood (for example, Matthew 26:26-27).

This study challenges us to grow closer to Christ by examining various aspects of Holy Communion. Specifically, we will reflect on its meaning in the following ways: as a prayer of thanksgiving, an active remembrance, an offering to God, a meal of spiritual nourishment, a communion with God and with others in Christ's name, a foretaste of the promised heavenly banquet, a call to service, and an act of praise to God, all of which are encapsulated in the idea of celebrating Emmanuel, "God with us." This is not an exhaustive list, but these are some aspects of Holy Communion that reveal its richness and depth while pointing us to the living presence of Jesus Christ in our lives. Along the way we will also explore how past, present, and future all intersect as we commune with God and with God's people. In addition, we will consider how this gift of God's grace engages the full range of human senses—seeing, hearing, smelling, touching, and tasting—as it gives us a share in the life of God and in Christ's mission in the world.

We experience the presence of Christ in many ways, but none more special, more intimate, more truly satisfying than in what is variously called Holy Communion, the Lord's Supper, or simply the Eucharist. Whatever name we use for it, this is a meal of God's grace that Christ has prepared for us. For it is here, as we respond in faith to his invitation, that he feeds our souls with the bread of life that endures forever. It is here, as we believe in him, that our spiritual thirst is quenched. It is here, as we partake of the bread and cup of the Lord's Supper, that we can say: The bread that we break is a sharing in the body of Christ, and the cup over which we give thanks is a sharing in the blood of Christ. It is here, in this holy meal, where God satisfies the deepest hunger and thirst of the human heart.

Why? Because here our souls feast upon and drink in a love so great that it will not let us go, a love that rescues us, forgives us, renews and restores us; a love so powerful that nothing, not even death, can separate us from it. It is all here, freely given for you, for me, for all people.

Questions for Reflection

1. In the introduction, we read: "To be human is to seek communion with something or someone, to seek happiness and meaning, to know and be known, and to love and be loved." What or who have you turned to in search of lasting fulfillment? What were the results? What kind of communion are you currently seeking, and for what purpose?

2. Do you think there is a connection between Holy Communion and a life of fulfillment, holiness, and peace? How has that been true for you, or how might it be?

3. How often does the church you attend or serve celebrate Holy Communion? In your local church, what seems to be the most common attitude toward Communion Sundays, or is it hard to say? If attendance or enthusiasm tends to differ on those Sundays compared to other Sundays, why do you think that is the case?

4. What is your current understanding of the significance of Holy Communion for the church and the Christian life? What do you hope to gain from this study?

Almighty God, you created us to experience true communion and fellowship with you and, in you, with others in this world. By your Spirit, help us open wide our hearts to you and abide in Christ by faith. Grant us to know the love and peace that Christ came to give, that love which is stronger than death and that peace which passes all understanding. We hunger and thirst, O God. You alone can satisfy. Give us the bread of life to eat, and quench our deep spiritual thirst as we believe in you. Speak to us and guide us throughout this study, and in all things; in the name of Jesus Christ we pray. Amen.

A Prayer of Thanksgiving: Seeking the Presence of God

Seek the LORD *while he may be found,*
call upon him while he is near;
let the wicked forsake their way,
and the unrighteous their thoughts;
let them return to the LORD, *that he may have mercy on them,*
and to our God, for he will abundantly pardon.

—Isaiah 55:6-7

The first time I walked into the church's prayer chapel, my heart sank. The dank, dimly lit room had become essentially a catchall. The walls were lined with boxes and dusty bookshelves overstuffed with old certificates, pictures, and other mementos (the congregation was gearing up for its 150th anniversary celebration). There were baskets of prayer request slips from services held years before. I don't even want to know how old the tissue box was! This space, once consecrated to God, was no longer used on a regular basis for the originally intended purpose. Instead it had become overrun with stuff, a lot of it junk.

There I was, the new pastor of a church that had a strong, proud heritage but more recently had experienced several decades of slow decline while nobly carrying on, a congregation like so many others these days. I was trying to envision through hope-filled eyes the potential for renewal and growth in that setting, but as I stepped into

1

the prayer chapel that day almost all I could see was a bunch of clutter in a space that was supposed to be devoted to prayer.

One way to gauge the vitality of a church is to look at the place of prayer in that church's life. The same is true on a personal level; the role of prayer in one's life probably gives a good indication of the depth, breadth, and power of that person's faith. God calls us to be a people of prayer, a people attentive to God's presence.

So easily, though, the stuff of our lives can spread and take over, as it did in that prayer chapel. We will likely find such a place in most churches, as well as most human hearts and lives—spaces or areas that were at one point dedicated to God and God's presence, but have since begun serving other purposes or no purpose at all. Without sufficient formation and care, without the light and order that we need, without remaining open to the fresh air of God's grace stirring among and within us, parts of our lives can become cluttered and musty, stifling rather than encouraging spiritual vitality.

Thankfully, God gives us the sacraments, sacred gifts endowed with divine power to clean up our lives. By these outward signs of an inward grace and God's goodwill toward us, the Holy Spirit works invisibly in us, and quickens, strengthens, and confirms our faith in Christ.[1] God authorizes and graciously imparts the sacraments to us for our sanctification. In his provocative treatise *The Babylonian Captivity of the Church*, Martin Luther identifies three essential elements of a sacrament: a divine promise, Christ's institution, and a physical sign. As we in the church today face our own captivity to the forces of shallow banalities, cultural accommodation, and debilitating apathy, what better place to turn than the sacraments? Sacraments are those signs whose substance conveys to us the promised presence of Jesus Christ to the glory of the Father through the power of the Holy Spirit. Baptism and the Eucharist are grounded in the activity of the triune God. As the medieval theologian Hugh of St. Victor explains, in the sacraments God sets before the external senses these physical or material elements that represent by likeness, signify by institution, and contain by sanctification some invisible and spiritual grace.[2] Through the waters of baptism God cleanses us, and through the Eucharist God feeds us and quenches our thirsty souls.

God with *Us*?

Before saying any more about what a sacrament is, though, and before focusing on the nature and purpose of the Lord's Supper in particular, we should return to the metaphor above about the cluttered space in our churches and lives that had once been devoted to God. The metaphor points to a deeper dilemma for us all: How can finite, messy, imperfect human beings encounter the infinite, perfectly holy God? What are human beings that God would want to be with us? For that to happen, surely God must make a way. The fundamental claim of the Christian faith is that God has made a way, a way through the one who called himself "the way, and the truth, and the life," Jesus Christ (John 14:6). Long before we ever thought to seek God, God had it in mind to come to us—and has done just that in Christ.

The saving benefits of Christ's coming into the world reach us as we believe and trust in him. He gives himself to us by his grace as a free, unmerited gift that we receive by faith. Before ascending into heaven, the risen Lord made this promise: "remember, I am with you always, to the end of the age" (Matthew 28:20). Jesus Christ is God with us, always and everywhere.

Thankfully, Christ's presence is not dependent on our actions. We do not need to have our lives all together for him to work in us. Taking the initiative, he meets us where we are. He met Peter and Andrew fishing and James and John mending their nets, and immediately they followed him (Matthew 4:18-22). Against the social customs of the day, he met the woman seeking a drink at Jacob's well in Samaria, and that encounter changed not only her life but also the lives of many others who believed in Jesus because of the woman's testimony (John 4:1-42). Jesus has a way of coming to us as we go about our daily activities as well. He comes to us and draws us to himself so that we, too, may follow him.

Before he would become one of the most influential figures of his era, as well as one of the great saints in the history of the church, Augustine was a young man enslaved by worldly desires. One day in a Milan garden, in the midst of a personal crisis, he was weeping in bitter agony when God spoke words of cleansing, freedom, and new life to his tortured, tainted soul. Augustine describes the events in this way:

> suddenly I heard a voice from the nearby house chanting as if it might be a boy or a girl (I do not know which), saying and repeating over and over again "Pick up and read, pick up and read." At once my countenance changed, and I began to think intently whether there might be some sort of children's game in which such a chant is used. But I could not remember having heard of one. I checked the flood of tears and stood up. I interpreted it solely as a divine command to me to open the book and read the first chapter I might find....So I hurried back to the place where...I had put down the book of the apostle when I got up. I seized it, opened it and in silence read the first passage on which my eyes lit.[3]

It was Romans 13:13-14: "Let us live honorably as in the day, not in reveling and drunkenness, not in debauchery and licentiousness, not in quarreling and jealousy. Instead, put on the Lord Jesus Christ, and make no provision for the flesh, to gratify its desires."

Augustine continues, "I neither wished nor needed to read further. At once, with the last words of this sentence, it was as if a light of relief from all anxiety flooded into my heart. All the shadows of doubt were dispelled."[4] The Lord came to him.

God Comes to Us through Grace

Jesus is the Word of God made flesh, God coming to us, God pursuing us. He reveals his presence more fully to us as we engage in specific practices designed and decreed by God, disciplines that deepen our discipleship, like Bible study and prayer. Christians throughout the ages have described such practices or disciplines using the phrase "means of grace." For example, John Wesley used that expression to denote those "outward signs, words, or actions ordained of God, and appointed...to be the *ordinary* channels" by which God conveys grace to us.[5]

What is grace? Grace is God's presence and power for us, in us, and through us. It is the unmerited favor and activity of God on our behalf, a gift, in Christ, that is beyond what we could ever deserve or even fully comprehend. Yet we can see its effects in our lives. By

> ## Grace is God's presence and power for us, in us, and through us. It is the unmerited favor and activity of God on our behalf, a gift.

grace, the Holy Spirit leads us on the way of salvation that is our journey back to God, our journey to becoming the people God calls us to be, or in short, our journey home.

Grace is free but not cheap. It is free to all people, in God's gracious providence, and is meant to be transformative for us as we respond in faith. The grace of God, however, is anything but cheap. Cheap "grace" (because it is only so-called grace) asks or demands nothing from us. Such "grace" is a fraudulent pretender, a disgraceful counterfeit. Yet it remains deceptively captivating to a church that is woefully undisciplined and, worse, undiscipled in the way of Christ. Cheap "grace" is not at all the grace of God, for this grace—truly divine grace—confronts us as a radical call to follow Jesus Christ, crucified and risen. As Dietrich Bonhoeffer wrote, and showed in his own life, the grace of God is costly.[6] The narrow road that leads to life is paved by grace, summoning us to submit fully to the lordship of Jesus Christ, who freely sacrificed everything for us all.

The command that God gives us through the prophet Isaiah pulsates with urgency: "Seek the LORD while he may be found, call upon him while he is near; let the wicked forsake their way, and the unrighteous their thoughts; let them return to the LORD, that he may have mercy on them, and to our God, for he will abundantly pardon" (Isaiah 55:6-7). We can seek and find God only because God has first sought and found us. God can be found in the means of grace because in these gifts and practices God promises to meet us, and unfailingly does.

Wesley cites three chief means of grace: "prayer, whether in se-
cret or with the great congregation; searching the Scriptures (which
implies reading, hearing, and meditating thereon), and receiving
the Lord's Supper, eating bread and drinking wine in remembrance
of him."[7] As Wesley goes on to explain, God is always above these
means. They have no power apart from God's action through them.
What makes these practices spiritually significant is that God meets
us here, as promised. They are channels of God's presence and power
graciously opened up to us by the living God, who invites us deeper
into a relationship of love with the one who is Love: the Father, the
Son, and the Holy Spirit.

The gifts that Wesley identifies as the three most important
means of grace—prayer, Scripture, and the Lord's Supper—all relate
to the order of worship that encompasses the actual receiving of the
bread and cup. In fact, the Eucharist is itself a prayer rooted in the
Scriptures. It is, in its entirety, a prayer of thanksgiving for the biblical saga of redemption, for all that God has done for us in creating
the world and redeeming it through Jesus Christ.

John Calvin articulates a similar perspective, reflecting on how
God's saving work for us evokes from faithful hearts a response that
is grounded in gratitude and expressed in the worship and service of
God. For Calvin as well, the meal is a gift of God, and like every gift,
it is an invitation to give thanks to the One who is the source of all
goodness, graciously revealed in Christ, as recounted in the scriptural
account of creation and redemption.[8]

Some experiences leave us so grateful that all we can say in response, whether aloud or in our hearts, is simply "Thank you. Thank
you." When our son was born following some difficult complications
with the pregnancy, Molly and I were overjoyed. All we could say was
"Thank you. Thank you." In the weeks and months that followed,
it was more like: "Thank you... and please, God, help us get more
sleep!"

In the Lord's Supper, we join our voices with the church from
across time and space in a continual prayer of thanksgiving. Viewing
the Lord's Supper for what it is, namely, a prayer thanking the God
of our salvation, brings into focus the profound spiritual meaning of

what is said and done during this part of worship. It is not an act to rush through but one to form us, deep within our hearts and lives. Communion is far from the empty ritual that some might see it as today. Instead, this gift of God's grace actually makes possible, for us, a fresh encounter with the living God.

A Journey through the Liturgy

The Invitation

As recounted in the liturgy (or order of worship) presented in *The United Methodist Hymnal*, the words of invitation to commune with Christ and with others in his name set the tone for what follows: "Christ our Lord invites to his table all who love him, who earnestly repent of their sin and seek to live in peace with one another. Therefore, let us confess our sin before God and one another."[9] Who doesn't like to be invited to a party or celebration? Receiving an invitation is like an affirmation that yes, I am included and invited. Out of love, Christ invites us all to come to him and find rest for our souls (Matthew 11:28-30). We respond to the Lord by faith and in prayer.

Confession and Pardon

Specifically, it is fitting for us to begin that response with a prayer of confession. Confession may be out of style in a largely therapeutic age, like our own, that teaches us to feel good about ourselves and to think the best about who we are and what we do and say. Nevertheless, if we truly wish to enter God's presence, then we had better come clean. The Scriptures teach us that basic point, as we see in the experience of the prophet Isaiah before the Lord. Isaiah's vision of God in the temple—"sitting on a throne, high and lofty" and surrounded by angels proclaiming that God is "holy, holy, holy"—overwhelmed the helpless prophet (Isaiah 6:1, 3). "The pivots on the thresholds shook at the voices of those who called, and the house filled with smoke. And I said: 'Woe is me! I am lost, for I am a man of unclean lips, and I live among a people of unclean lips; yet my eyes have seen the King, the LORD of hosts!' " (Isaiah 6:4-5). Later, the coal cleansed Isaiah's lips. His sin was forgiven, and he was sent forth to serve as a representative of God. For us, too, standing in the presence of almighty God should have the same effect, leading us to exclaim, "Woe is me!"

While God used the coal to cleanse Isaiah's lips, in a similar way the use of ashes as a sign of our mortality and repentance has a long history in Jewish and Christian worship. For Christians, Ash Wednesday is a call to repentance and reconciliation. One woman was facing difficulties on several fronts, including the ongoing grief over the death of her husband and the challenges of battling health issues of her own. It was enough to weigh her down spiritually, and she was struggling with bitterness and despair. She came to our church's worship on Ash Wednesday and received the imposition of ashes on her forehead in the sign of the cross. She shared in Holy Communion. Through it all God used that experience to renew her mind and heart by drawing her closer to Christ and his cross in an especially meaningful way. Weeks later she remarked, "Ever since the Ash Wednesday service, I have felt like a totally new person on the inside." The difference was perceptible on the outside, too, as others in the church noticed a change in her demeanor. For a long time she had tried to hold herself together on the inside, and then she came to realize, through an encounter with God, that there is nothing we can hide. Jesus wants us to come to him as we are, not just if we have our lives in order.

The prayer of confession represents a candid, sobering acknowledgment that before God, all our pain and brokenness are exposed, and we are fully known. One person who regularly attended worship would intentionally stay home whenever the church celebrated the Lord's Supper. He explained his rationale for skipping worship on Communion Sundays by saying, "I just don't feel like I have that much to confess." He apparently thought, perhaps as others have as well, that the meaning of Communion was reduced to the confession of our sins. Ironically, by justifying his absence with a claim of having not "that much to confess," he sounded awfully prideful. Plus, that is no excuse to miss out on what is happening when the church gathers for the Lord's Supper. Confession is a critical component, but there is more to the service of Communion than mere confession. Ultimately, the purpose of confession is not for self-loathing but for God's glory and for our good, that we may be restored to right relationship with God. By confessing our sins, we humble ourselves before God and ask God to forgive us, heal us, and raise us up to live a new and better life.

So as we prepare to commune with God, the church teaches us to pray, "Merciful God, we confess that we have not loved you with our whole heart."[10] In Mark 12:29-30, Jesus, quoting the first commandment from Moses in Deuteronomy 6:4-5, states that the first and greatest commandment is the *Shema* (Hebrew for "hear"): "Hear, O Israel: the Lord our God, the Lord is one; you shall love the Lord your God with all your heart, and with all your soul, and with all your mind, and with all your strength." We should be fully devoted to God, but so often our love for God falls far short of this standard.

The confession continues, "We have failed to be an obedient church."[11] In the book of Revelation, the Lord conveys a message to the church in various places. That message speaks to the problem of disobedience, which we struggle with still today. Like the church in Ephesus, we have in various ways abandoned the love we had at first (Revelation 2:4). Like the church in Sardis, we need to be awakened from a state of spiritual slumber (Revelation 3:1-3). Like it did for the church in Laodicea, material prosperity, particularly for so many Christians in America, conceals if not induces a spiritual poverty and feebleness; and so we boast of being rich and prosperous, needing nothing, while overlooking our true state—"wretched, pitiable, poor, blind, and naked" (Revelation 3:17). As in every age, even now the Word of God stands above the world, shatters our self-constructed façades of righteousness, reveals the truth of our compromised condition, and calls us to account. Jesus lamented over Jerusalem, "How often have I desired to gather your children together as a hen gathers her brood under her wings, and you were not willing!" (Matthew 23:37). By confessing our sins, we admit our own unwillingness to be gathered together in the arms of Jesus. That admission implicitly expresses the hope that, strengthened by God's grace, we might become more receptive and responsive to what the Lord desires.

There is more for us to say before God about our failure to obey, with each phrase again rooted in Scripture: "We have not done your will." One of the petitions in the Lord's Prayer is "your will be done" (Matthew 6:10), but often we prefer our will to God's. "We have broken your law." The coming of Christ has not done away with God's law but fulfilled it (Matthew 5:17), though we willingly violate God's sacred teaching and live as if it did not matter. "We have rebelled against your love." Christ plainly says, "This is my commandment, that you love one another as I have loved you. No one has greater love than this, to lay down one's life for one's friends" (John 15:12-13). We confess, as the prayer continues, that we "have not loved our neighbors." We have stopped short of showing consistent, genuine love for others, especially those in need, though according to Jesus the second greatest commandment of all is this, "You shall love your neighbor as yourself" (Mark 12:31, quoting Leviticus 19:18). So we pray, "We have not heard the cry of the needy." We have, by and large, not responded as we should toward "the least of these who are members of [Christ's] family" (Matthew 25:40), and our inadequate response toward them amounts to a denial of Christ himself (see Matthew 25:31-46). For these reasons and others, it is not only appropriate but incumbent upon us to confess our sins before God and one another.[12]

A friend of mine had the courage and faith to pray this prayer: "God, if there are parts of my life that you don't like, chip away at them until they crumble and disintegrate." Sure enough, she found in the following weeks and months that Jesus was chipping away at those parts of her life that were not pleasing to him. She was being refined by the refiner's fire. That purging was sometimes uncomfortable, but she had prayed that God would do this. My friend admitted that sometimes she said to herself, "Why did I pray that prayer?" She almost wished she had played it safe and not prayed like that after all. Later, though, she came to see that through that prayer God was molding and shaping her character. As she explained, God was helping her be more accepting of others and welcoming toward them. God's response to her prayer revealed to her some additional confession that was necessary in her life.

Each of us would do well to ask: "What have I done, said, and thought that is not pleasing to God? Are there edges in my life that need to be chipped away and smoothed out?" Through prayer and confession, God will continually refine us.

After naming what alienates us from God and others, we appeal for God's mercy and deliverance: "Forgive us, we pray." We pray that Christ, out of the abundance of his mercy, would forgive and restore us, like he forgave and restored Peter who also denied him by his words and actions (John 21:15-19). "Free us for joyful obedience, through Jesus Christ our Lord." This part of the preparation to receive the Eucharist—this corporate prayer drawing from the very marrow of the Bible's message—concludes with reference to the transformative power of God's grace in Jesus Christ. The one who alone is in a position to condemn, Jesus Christ, still forgives sinners and calls us, like he did the woman of old, to go and sin no more (John 8:11).[13]

Through confession, we tap into a power to love that is vastly greater than anything we possess or could muster up on our own. Corrie ten Boom once encountered a former Nazi prison guard whom she remembered from the concentration camp where she had been held captive. Her family had been arrested for hiding Jews in their home during the Nazi occupation of Holland. She and her sister Betsie were sent to Ravensbrück concentration camp, where this man was a guard. Betsie was one of the many people who died in that place of intense suffering.

Several years later, Corrie saw the man again in a church in Munich. It was 1947, and she had come from Holland to vanquished, dilapidated Germany in order to share the message of God's forgiveness. She declared to all who would listen that when we confess our sins, God forgives them and throws them into the deepest sea so that they are gone forever. After her talk, the people filed out in somber silence, except for one man who, "beaming and bowing," came forward to speak to her.[14] It was the former prison guard. The mere sight of that man brought back dreadful memories for Corrie, including the shame of having to strip down and walk naked past him. Of course, she thought of Betsie as well.

That same man now stood in front of her. He held out his hand to her and spoke up: "A fine message, Fräulein! How good it is to know that, as you say, all our sins are at the bottom of the sea!"[15] She did not think he could possibly remember her, one prisoner among the thousands of women, but she certainly remembered him, one of her former captors. Rather than take his hand, she awkwardly rooted around in her pocketbook. He went on to explain that after serving as a guard at Ravensbrück he had become a Christian. He said that he knew God had forgiven him for the sins he committed there, but he wanted to seek Corrie's forgiveness as well. Once more he extended his hand toward her, and then he asked plainly whether she, too, would forgive him.

The seconds seemed like hours as Corrie struggled mightily to do what she knew she must do—forgive. But Betsie had died in that horrible place, she thought. Could this man "erase her slow terrible death simply for the asking?"[16] The inner battle intensified, and it shook Corrie to her core. Later she would write: "Even as the angry, vengeful thoughts boiled through me, I saw the sin of them. Jesus Christ had died for this man; was I going to ask for more? 'Lord Jesus,' I prayed, 'forgive me and help me to forgive him.'"[17] Corrie tried to smile, though it was in vain. She strained to raise her hand but could not. She "felt nothing, not the slightest spark of warmth or charity."[18] She stood there with her hand at her side and her heart clutched by coldness. But as she had told others, "forgiveness is not an emotion—I knew that too. Forgiveness is an act of the will, and the will can function regardless of the temperature of the heart."[19] Corrie had taught many others about forgiveness, but here she was facing a very difficult lesson of her own.

Again she breathed a silent prayer: "Jesus, I cannot forgive him. Give me Your forgiveness."[20] Then she finally managed to thrust her hand into the one stretched out to her. This is how she describes what happened as she took his hand: "From my shoulder along my arm and through my hand a current seemed to pass from me to him, while into my heart sprang a love for this stranger that almost over-whelmed me."[21] A sensation of healing warmth filled her whole being and brought tears to her eyes. "'I forgive you, brother!' I cried. 'With all my heart!' For a long moment we grasped each other's hands, the former guard and the former prisoner. I had never known God's love so intensely as I did then."[22]

Forgiveness and love have a vertical dimension pertaining to our relationship with God. They also have a horizontal dimension that pertains to our relationships with other people. Those two dimensions intersect in the form of a cross, the ultimate symbol of what God has done to redeem us in Christ.

As much as, in our pride, we might wish to skip over confession or pretend there is no need to confess, in the acknowledgment of our sinfulness and brokenness, there is good news for us all. During the service of Holy Communion, following the corporate confession and prayers of personal confession in silence, the word of the gospel breaks through: "Christ died for us while we were yet sinners; that proves God's love toward us. In the name of Jesus Christ, you are forgiven!" The people repeat the news because it is too good not to share: "In the name of Jesus Christ, you are forgiven!"[23]

When has something so great happened to you that you simply had to spread the word? Perhaps it was the birth of a child, or a job promotion, or even the thrill of winning an exciting game (the meaning of which is not lost on my wife, Molly, who loves to play tennis). Good news is meant to be shared. The gospel is good news, as the very meaning of the word denotes. Certainly, the message of God's forgiveness for us in Christ warrants a joyful response from thankful hearts, overflowing in gratitude and praise to God.

The Peace and Offering

That is what this portion of the liturgy aims to facilitate. After hearing the good news of forgiveness in Jesus Christ, the pastor and people declare together, "Glory to God. Amen."[24] Then, as forgiven and reconciled people, we exchange signs and words of God's peace, and offer ourselves and our gifts to God. There is always the pos-sibility of merely going through the motions here, as elsewhere in worship, but when we reflect on these words and actions, we can gain a greater appreciation of their significance, and in that way come to participate more fully in the church's praise of God.

Taking the Bread and Cup

Up to this point in worship, we have confessed our sins, received God's word of pardon, shared in the peace, and offered ourselves and our gifts anew to God. We are now prepared for the next step toward deeper closeness with God. Now the pastor and people are ready to engage in a fourfold movement that draws us all into the presence of God through the gift of Holy Communion. It is a movement patterned after the actions of Jesus himself, who took bread, blessed it, broke it, and gave it to his disciples (see, for example, Mark 14:22).

First, the pastor takes the bread and cup, and prepares them for the meal. For all that we have experienced of God's presence so far, there is more yet to come. As the sight of the bread and cup signifies, the one who is God with us prepares a place for us, for the refreshment of our souls.

The Great Thanksgiving

Second, for the blessing of the elements, the pastor and people celebrate what is often called the Great Thanksgiving. This is all a prayer, and it begins with the traditional call to prayer. "The Lord be with you," says the pastor, invoking the presence of God. The people respond, "And also with you" (or in some versions of the prayer, "And with thy spirit"). The pastor continues, once more addressing the people, "Lift up your hearts." The response indicates the true recipient of these words of prayer, "We lift them up to the Lord." With our hearts lifted up to the Lord, we "give thanks to the Lord our God."[25]

Then the pastor addresses God directly, in a sweeping summary of salvation history:

> It is right, and a good and joyful thing, always and everywhere to give thanks to you, Father Almighty, creator of heaven and earth.

You formed us in your image and breathed into us the breath of life. When we turned away, and our love failed, your love remained steadfast. You delivered us from captivity, made covenant to be our sovereign God, and spoke to us through your prophets. And so, with your people on earth and all the company of heaven we praise your name and join their unending hymn.[26]

This story becomes our story, and we can identify with both the triumphs and the struggles of God's people across the ages. We can see from our own lives as well the significance of remembering in this way. Consider, for example, the life and legacy of Rosa Parks. She worked prophetically to right a wrong—the societal injustice of racial discrimination—and was motivated in large part by her Christian faith. The church was a primary institution to which Parks remained committed unto death. Its story of God's deliverance had guided and inspired the life of this woman, a life that had, in turn, inspired others. At Parks's viewing in Montgomery, Alabama, in 2005, "Condoleezza Rice…affirmed that 'without Mrs. Parks, I probably would not be standing here today as Secretary of State.'"[27] In Communion, we claim the history of God's salvation as our own, or perhaps more aptly we are claimed by that defining story, and we are called by God to live it in our own day and age.

During the service of the Lord's Supper, together all the people lift their voices, "Holy, holy, holy Lord, God of power and might, heaven and earth are full of your glory. Hosanna in the highest. Blessed is he who comes in the name of the Lord. Hosanna in the highest," echoing the chorus of praise sung by the angels in Isaiah's vision of God (see Isaiah 6:3).[28] There are two noteworthy allusions to Jesus in those words. First, the term *Hosanna*, meaning "save" or "rescue," was the shout of praise made in recognition of Jesus as the Messiah on his triumphal entry into Jerusalem: "Hosanna! Blessed is the one who comes in the name of the Lord! Blessed is the coming kingdom of our ancestor David! Hosanna in the highest heaven!" (Mark 11:9-10). Christians remember that event each year on Palm Sunday, usually marked by a ritual reenactment of how people lined the streets of Jerusalem, spread their cloaks on the road, and waved leafy branches from the fields as they welcomed Jesus. Here in the

Lord's Supper, those words help us welcome Jesus our Savior and recognize his presence among us still today.

In Matthew's Gospel, a mere two chapters after Jesus enters Jerusalem, the Lord issues a scathing critique of the scribes and Pharisees, the religious leaders, by calling them "blind guides" and, repeatedly, "hypocrites" (Matthew 23:16; 13, 15, 23, 25, 27, 29). He chastises the people as a whole for their unwillingness to be gathered together by him, and then quotes the Psalmist, "For I tell you, you will not see me again until you say, 'Blessed is the one who comes in the name of the Lord'" (Matthew 23:39; Psalm 118:26). Uniquely and decisively, Jesus is the one who comes in the Lord's name. He is the Lord, and he has come to us and is with us now. That is what this prayer of thanksgiving commemorates.

What was implied before, in the words up to this point, deserves to be clearly proclaimed: God's actions in creation and redemption reach their wondrous climax in Jesus Christ, the Savior of the world. He is God's Word made flesh, the unmitigated revelation of God to us, for us, and with us.

During my first visit to Rome, I did not think my trip would be complete without the purchase of an icon. Anyone who has been to Rome knows firsthand that there is no shortage of icon options there. I found one I liked, got the shopkeeper's attention, and pointed to the image I wanted to buy, which depicted Jesus holding the Bible. There were so many icons in the store that the man mistakenly thought I had pointed to an image of Jesus holding a closed Bible. So he climbed up on the ladder and began taking that one down for me. I wanted to buy the one right next to it, with Jesus holding and pointing to an open Bible rather than a closed one. In broken Italian I said to the shopkeeper as I motioned, "No, open." They were both visually appealing images, but I wanted the one in particular for theological reasons. Jesus not only points to the Scriptures; he opens up the Scriptures. He unlocks the truth of which he himself is the key.[29] As he did with the two sojourners on the Emmaus road, Jesus teaches us the things about himself in the Scriptures (Luke 24:27). He opens the Scriptures to us so that our hearts might burn with us (Luke 24:32). Just as surely, he makes himself known, like he did for those two so long ago, in the breaking and blessing of the bread (Luke 24:30-31).

In the service of Holy Communion, the church's prayer begins to concentrate explicitly on the person at the center of our faith: "Holy are you, and blessed is your Son Jesus Christ." In his person and work, Jesus brings God's salvation to our world and establishes the kingdom of God here and now by his presence and power. "Your Spirit anointed him to preach good news to the poor, to proclaim release to the captives and recovering of sight to the blind, to set at liberty those who are oppressed, and to announce that the time had come when you would save your people." At the start of his ministry, Jesus summarized his mission by quoting these words from Isaiah 61:1-2 and then announcing that this Scripture has been fulfilled in him (see Luke 4:16-21). Jesus, the prayer of thanksgiving continues, "healed the sick, fed the hungry, and ate with sinners"—actions central to his ministry (see, for example, John 4:43-54; Matthew 14:15-21; and Mark 2:13-17). The upshot of what Christ has done is the formation of a community of God's people, the church, as in this allusion to Romans 6:3-14: "By the baptism of his suffering, death, and resurrection you gave birth to your church, delivered us from slavery to sin and death, and made with us a new covenant by water and the Spirit." Then we hear once more, fittingly, the abiding promise made by Jesus before he ascended to heaven: "When the Lord Jesus ascended, he promised to be with us always, in the power of your Word and Holy Spirit" (see Matthew 28:20).[30]

That promise leads to a further sharpening of the focus as the institution of the Lord's Supper is celebrated.

On the night in which he gave himself up for us, he took bread, gave thanks to you, broke the bread, gave it to his disciples, and said: "Take, eat; this is my body which is given for you. Do this in remembrance of me." When the supper was over, he took the cup, gave thanks to you, gave it to his disciples, and said: "Drink from this, all of you; this is my blood of the new covenant, poured out for you and for many for the forgiveness of sins. Do this, as often as you drink it, in remembrance of me."[31]

17

God's self-giving in Jesus Christ—withholding nothing and giving everything, even his own life—demands our own self-giving, as reflected in these words: "And so, in remembrance of these your mighty acts in Jesus Christ, we offer ourselves in praise and thanksgiving as a holy and living sacrifice, in union with Christ's offering for us, as we proclaim the mystery of faith." Together, the people summarize our faith in three short but potent phrases, "Christ has died; Christ is risen; Christ will come again."[32]

> God's saving work in Christ is a mystery that our faith allows us to discern, embrace, and grow to understand more fully even if we can never completely comprehend its inexhaustible splendor.

This is a mystery not in the sense of an unsolvable riddle or puzzle, or a matter about which we have no idea. Rather, God's saving work in Christ is a mystery that our faith allows us to discern, embrace, and grow to understand more fully even if we can never completely comprehend its inexhaustible splendor. Yet there are many people today, including some in the church, who do not know much about Jesus Christ and what he has done, or about what C. S. Lewis famously calls "mere Christianity."[33] When one British hospital chaplain asked people "Would you like Holy Communion?" he received these replies: "No thanks, I'm Church of England." "No thanks, I asked for Cornflakes." "No thanks, I've never been circumcised."[34] The claims of Christianity might sound irrelevant and undesirable when a basic understanding is lacking, but appropriate instruction and formation can, through the work of the Holy Spirit, lead others to see the wisdom of God revealed in Jesus Christ. The Eucharist, like our faith itself, revolves around the grandeur of the incarnation. That is what we affirm as we prepare to commune with Christ and with his people.

Then the pastor invokes the power of the Holy Spirit's blessing to make real all that God has promised to bestow on the faithful through Holy Communion.

> Pour out your Holy Spirit on us gathered here, and on these gifts of bread and wine. Make them be for us the body and blood of Christ, that we may be for the world the body of Christ, redeemed by his blood. By your Spirit make us one with Christ, one with each other, and one in ministry to all the world, until Christ comes in final victory and we feast at his heavenly banquet. Through your Son Jesus Christ, with the Holy Spirit in your holy church, all honor and glory is yours, almighty Father, now and for ever.[35]

This portion of the prayer highlights a profound truth of the Christian faith: Through the Eucharist, the Holy Spirit brings us into union with God and therefore with one another in the service of Christ. The people, in faithful approval of this request, say "Amen," which means "May it be so," often followed by the Lord's Prayer.[36] So after the pastor takes the bread and cup in the first of four phases preparing us to commune with Christ, the words quoted above represent our joining of Jesus's own prayer—his prayer when he instituted this sacrament—in the second movement of the liturgy of Holy Communion, blessing those elements with thanksgiving.

Breaking the Bread

Next, in the third stage of this prayer of thanksgiving, the pastor breaks the bread, often while saying, "Because there is one loaf, we, who are many, are one body, for we all partake of the one loaf. The bread which we break is a sharing in the body of Christ" (see 1 Corinthians 10:16-17). The pastor lifts the cup in silence or while saying, "The cup over which we give thanks is a sharing in the blood of Christ" (see 1 Corinthians 10:16). The lifting of the consecrated elements corresponds to the lifting of our prayers before the throne of God, including this prayer of thanksgiving for all that God has done, is doing, and will do for us in Christ. Ushered by prayer into the presence of God, we see in the breaking of the bread and lifting of the cup a visual reminder that at the heart of God's life is self-giving love, broken and poured out for us and for the life of the world.[37]

Giving the Bread and Cup

Since all things have now been made ready, we come to the fourth and final movement of the Communion liturgy, the giving of the bread and cup. In these sacred moments, the bread and wine are given to the people, accompanied by two simple phrases that speak of a mystery truly divine: "The body of Christ, given for you. The blood of Christ, given for you."[38] *This is a high point in the life of the church, and in our lives as believers.* Here our search for God finds its earthly fulfillment. Here, by tasting and drinking of God's abundant goodness, we experience the presence of God with us. Here we encounter God because God has chosen first to come to us in Christ. Communion with God is holy, set apart, since God, the object and agent of our communion, is holy. In the midst of the sheer holiness of this part of worship, the congregation sings or prays silently while the bread and cup are given. When all have received, the Lord's altar is put in order.

Given for All, Received with Gratitude

This is a feast not just for some, but for the whole church, as shown in several practical ways. Those who prepare the elements, by first obtaining them and then setting them in place before worship, often go unnoticed. But these people have a particularly important role to play on behalf of the congregation. For one volunteer, Communion Sunday was a highlight for her family, in part because after worship they all gladly consumed the extra consecrated bread (that is fine, according to tradition). Her children would often say that no other bread tasted quite as good as Communion bread. In another case, one young man helped bake the bread that would be used during the Eucharist on the day he was confirmed. Because the church kitchen was right beneath the sanctuary, the flavorful aroma rose from the kitchen and spread tantalizingly throughout the sanctuary that morning. In addition, many churches send visitation teams to share Communion with shut-in members of the church, often using the same elements from worship that morning. That practice beautifully manifests our unity in Christ, as members of one body in him.

Equipped and Empowered for Self-Giving Love

In the liturgy, the following prayer expresses our gratitude for this means of grace, as well as the petition that the fellowship we have experienced here with God and one another will influence how we live as servants of God: "Eternal God, we give you thanks for this holy mystery in which you have given yourself to us. Grant that we may go into the world in the strength of your Spirit, to give ourselves for others, in the name of Jesus Christ our Lord. Amen."[39] Through the Holy Spirit, God's gifts to us in the suffering, redemptive love of Jesus equip and empower us for lives of self-giving love in Jesus's name.

Hymn, Dismissal, and Blessing

Finally, after a hymn or song, the people are sent forth with a blessing from 2 Corinthians 13:13 reminding them of the presence of God. "Go forth in peace. The grace of the Lord Jesus Christ, and the love of God, and the communion of the Holy Spirit be with you all. Amen."[40] What happens in worship and especially in the Eucharist takes us to the heart of the Christian life. At its essential core that life is a sharing, through the Holy Spirit, in the life and love of God made flesh in Jesus Christ.

Remember and Celebrate God's Life with Us, Then and Now

With that, our journey through the liturgy, which draws us deep into the heart of God, is complete. Certainly, however, to use these exact words is by no means the only way to celebrate the Eucharist. Other church traditions use their own specific formulations and order. There is in many cases a striking theological similarity across church traditions, reflecting the findings of ancient Christian documents that indicate that the early Christians used language much like this as they worshiped God and participated in the Lord's Supper. Christians have a distinctive, peculiar language that helps us discover and worship God. The main concern for our purposes here is not really which specific words are used and how. What matters most is the deeper reality to which those words point—the reality of God's own life given to us in the bread and cup of the Lord. Through the service of Holy Communion, we remember and celebrate all that Christ gives us in this meal, particularly the gift of his grace, his presence and power for, in, and through us.

The words cited above show that the celebration of Holy Communion encompasses all three of what Wesley called the chief means of grace. It includes prayer because it all takes place in the context of prayer and, in fact, as a prayer of thanksgiving to the God of our salvation. This sacramental encounter with God's presence and power incorporates Scripture because it repeats the major themes of the Bible, stretching from the creation of the world to its redemption in Jesus Christ, as demonstrated by a number of scriptural quotations and allusions. Of course, the Lord's Supper is precisely what is happening here because this sacred ceremony culminates in our communion with Christ and with others in him. Prayer, Scripture, and the Eucharist are all interwoven in the experience of receiving the gifts given to us here by God. It is a prayer of thanksgiving that prepares us to encounter the God of Scripture in fresh and life-giving ways through the great feast of our faith, Holy Communion.

Physical and Spiritual Renovation

At the beginning of this chapter, I mentioned the prayer chapel at the church I have served since July 2010. That space looks much different now than what I described earlier. It has been cleaned, updated, and renovated. The clutter has been removed and the space is once again used regularly for its intended purpose; it is a place of prayer. Against the back wall now stands a beautifully restored painting of Jesus praying in the Garden of Gethsemane. That painting, which poignantly conveys the emotion of those moments, holds special significance for this church because it was used in the sanctuary of the church's old building. The painting in the prayer chapel represents the link between past and present for this congregation, while reminding all who see it of the connection that we all share with one another, and especially with God, through prayer.

This church's prayer chapel is rather small, with room for only about twenty people. The room does get quite cozy when it is at or near full capacity. Yet in the mystery of God's kingdom, the power of prayer is not measured in size or numbers as much as in depth. The transformation of our prayer chapel symbolizes a much deeper reality. That space has become, more than any other part of the church building, a visual representation of the renewal that God has brought to the congregation. It is a renewal rooted in a more frequent and attentive use of the means of grace, especially prayer, Scripture, and the Eucharist.

A Closer Walk

In the fall of 2010, the church began offering, in our prayer chapel, a midweek service of Communion. That simple, informal service has contributed to the resurgence of a congregation that had been—like so many other local churches—experiencing decades of decline. Our midweek service has never attracted a large group (rarely more than twelve people), but the impact has been palpable in our midst. Each week we gather to hear God's word, to sing, to celebrate the Eucharist, and to pray. We pray for those on our church prayer list. We ask God to expand our church's reach and grow our ministries to carry out Christ's mission in our community. We pray for those who suffer and those in trouble, and we ask God to renew and bless our church as well as the wider church so that we might be, more and more, a beacon of light, peace, and hope in the world. God has used that weekly gathering to help breathe new life into this church and to revitalize this congregation from the inside out. The fruit has been clear and consistent, including steady and substantial increases in worship attendance, giving, support of missions, and service to the community. When people pray, things start to happen![41]

Catalyst for Spiritual Renewal

More frequent celebration of the presence of Jesus Christ—God with us—in Holy Communion is one way to begin laying the groundwork for renewal within our churches. The Lord's Supper, this prayer of thanksgiving to the God of our salvation, brings us to the table where we must confess our sins, hear the gospel message again and again, and actually respond to it by receiving the gift of Christ's presence. Since we have instituted weekly Communion at this church, those who come to the midweek service have formed deeper bonds of friendship and love with one another. Often, they now meet for dinner before worship, and the spirit of fellowship and joy from their shared meal aptly flows into our time of worship and Communion.

The service has been a catalyst for spiritual renewal throughout the church, which is itself an answer to our weekly prayers. As a church, we started to become a more vibrant, grace-filled community right around the time we implemented the practice of midweek Eucharist. One person who first visited our church a short time later, and who has since become a member of our church family, recently told me how thankful she was for the difference that the church has made in her life. She said, "I want to thank God for these people who have brought peace into my life." She went on to mention several people by name including one woman who had first invited her to our Wednesday worship, which she now regularly attends.

Common Need for Grace

Celebrating weekly Communion has helped us begin to experience, in the way of humility and the peace of the Lord, an increased awareness of our common need for grace and of God's healing mercies in Christ, as well as a greater sense of warmth that continues to spread throughout our congregation's life. Like every congregation and every Christian, we are on a journey and have not yet reached our destination. However, the way to full and final union with God is set clearly before us as we experience and respond to God's presence in our lives, a presence that we tangibly encounter in the gift of Holy Communion. That same gift of God's grace is available for other congregations, and I believe that in one way or another, under the gracious providence of God, those same results will follow. The fruit of the Spirit is the fruit of authentic fellowship with God.

Feeding Souls

As most pastors know—and lament—low worship attendance or enthusiasm often accompanies Communion Sundays. That tendency alone might discourage overworked, numbers-mindful pastors from seeing the Lord's Supper as a key to formation and renewal. It is tempting for a pastor to wonder, "If I offered the sacrament more regularly, would 'enough' people show up and actually come ready to commune with God?" But it is not simply great preaching that will feed the souls of our people, many of whom hunger for more. While preaching is essential for proclaiming the word of God, the Eucharist gives us the opportunity to respond to the Lord in concrete, physical ways.

For pastors and church leaders, one practical, proven step toward greater spiritual vigor among and through the people in the congregation is to implement a midweek service of prayer and use that service as an entry point for increased practice of the Eucharist. This formula is not original to me or to this church setting. Actually, it derives from the witness of the early church, whose members regularly broke bread together and, empowered by the Holy Spirit, lived out their mission for Jesus Christ in transformative ways (see Acts 2:42-47). The main argument throughout these pages is that faithful participation in the Lord's Supper grounds us in God's love and leads to growth and renewal.

Greater Obedience to and Deeper Friendship with Christ

Wesley spoke of "the duty of constant communion" in a sermon of that name, a sermon title adapted from a text by Robert Nelson called *The Great Duty of Frequenting the Christian Sacrifice*.[42] Not content with the idea of "frequent communion," Wesley argues in this sermon that it is the duty of every Christian to receive the Lord's Supper as often as possible. Because Christ commands us to do this (for example, Luke 22:19), and because of the benefits that we thus receive, our communion with Christ in the Eucharist is to be so determinative and abiding as to be "constant," according to Wesley. How far we have come from such a vision of the Christian life! Is it any wonder that so many of our churches, and our people, are spiritually depleted?

But to be clear, what I am proposing here is not a quick fix for church growth. This is not one more slickly designed program or process to attract people in an age of material and spiritual consumerism. Instead, I have in mind something different. I am issuing a call for greater obedience to Christ and deeper friendship with him and with others in his name. I do so in the firm conviction that our union with God by grace through faith, a union that is realized in a special way in the Eucharist, will not only change us but also use us to make disciples of Christ and impact the world for God's glory.

The church needs to reclaim its commitment to faithful, active, joyful participation in the sacrament of Holy Communion, understood for what it truly is—neither a dull and basically meaningless ritual nor an optional extra for those so inclined, but in fact a fresh and formative encounter for one and all with the risen Christ himself. In order to become more fully alive in Christ, we should be certain to use to its full extent this great gift that God has given us in the Lord's Supper, an untapped well of authentic spirituality and the promise of hope made real to us through the living presence of Jesus Christ.

There are many helpful resources available to pastors and lay people as they seek a renewed and growing spiritual vitality in their own daily lives and throughout their churches and wider communities. However, could it be that what we need most of all is simply a greater attentiveness to God, and to those primary means of grace that we call prayer, Scripture, and Holy Communion? Could it be that in encountering anew the presence and power of almighty God, especially through the Supper of the Lord, we might be increasingly drawn into the life-giving work of the Holy Spirit? Could it be that all we need in order to live in the abundance of Christ's love is already given to us? As we read in the Psalms, those timeless prayers of God's people, "Taste and see that the Lord is good; happy are those who take refuge in him" (34:8).

Questions for Reflection

1. Share your most meaningful Communion experience.

2. What difference does it make to claim that in order for us to encounter the presence of God, God must first make a way for us (in other words, finding God is not something we could ever do on our own, apart from God's initiative and guidance)? Why is that a spiritually significant point?

3. When and how have you seen God at work in your life? How has God used the practices of prayer, reading Scripture, and receiving Holy Communion to deepen your faith and contribute to your spiritual growth?

4. Are there any aspects of your life that are like the prayer chapel mentioned in this chapter—areas that were once consecrated to God but have since become neglected? How can you reclaim those areas for God's purposes?

5. Have you ever stopped to think about the meaning of the words used in Communion services at your church? What do those words say about God, the world, and the purposes of God? What do they suggest about how we can encounter and live for God?

6. Write a prayer of thanksgiving for what God has done in your life, and how the presence of God has been graciously revealed to you. As a way of preparation, pray that prayer silently shortly before the next time you receive the Lord's Supper, such as the morning of worship or the night before.

Loving God, in you we live, move, and have our being. It is always good to give thanks to you, for you are the Lord our God. Forgive us for all that keeps us from following your ways wholeheartedly. Draw us closer to Christ, and breathe your Holy Spirit upon us once more. Order our lives, good Lord, that our souls may be refreshed and strengthened for your service; through Jesus Christ our Savior, who is God with us now and always. Amen.

Chapter 2

Remembering Christ's Presence with Us

For as often as you eat this bread and drink the cup, you proclaim the Lord's death until he comes.

—1 Corinthians 11:26

During my first semester of seminary, the Introduction to Old Testament class was held in the chapel. As students anxiously walked into class on the first day, copies of the course syllabus—dozens of thick pages, detailing assignment after assignment—were stacked on the altar, directly above the words inscribed on the altar's wood, "Do this in remembrance of me." It was an odd juxtaposition. With all the work before us to do, my classmates and I wondered what exactly we had gotten ourselves into, in the name of Jesus.

When it comes to our life with the God who made heaven and earth, the God revealed in Jesus Christ, remembering is not a mere passive activity. God calls us to an active remembrance, to remember by doing, in the name of Jesus.

Communion occupies a central place in the Christian faith, which is all about our communion or fellowship with God through Jesus Christ and with one another in Christ. But often Holy Communion, which offers the most tangible experience of that fellowship in this world, is something that we may take for granted. We may not think much about the true meaning of Communion for our life today. I am speaking from experience; when I was growing up, I used to think that Communion was by far the most boring thing of all the boring things that we did at church. I would have much rather looked at my baseball cards—and sometimes did, even in church (to the dismay of my Sunday school teachers).

The previous chapter focused on how Holy Communion is itself a prayer. It is a prayer of thanksgiving for who God is and for all that God has done for us in Jesus Christ. For that reason, Communion is also a remembrance of the Last Supper. Jesus commands his disciples to do this in remembrance of him (Luke 22:19; 1 Corinthians 11:24-25). The memorial nature of the sacrament makes it an active recalling of Christ's final meal with the disciples. For most people in our churches today, this is probably the default mode of thinking about Communion. However, what happens in the Eucharist is much more than an empty memorialism. We remember what Christ has said and done for us not simply as past events that are forever behind us, but instead as completed actions with ongoing significance and impact.

The Power of Remembering

Once during a children's message, I asked a group of kids from the church what their first memory was. The responses came quickly: "I remember what I had for breakfast this morning." "I remember when my little brother was born." Then, as if to top the others, a young boy eagerly spoke up: "I remember being born." Part of the fun of moments with children is having no idea what the kids might say. Their comments often add humor and joy to our worship.

One of my earliest and most enduring memories involves the birth of my younger sister. My parents chose to have the birth at home with the help of a midwife. As it happened, the babysitter could not come that day due to a major snowstorm, which meant that my older sister and I were on our own for part of the time. At ages five and three, respectively, Emily and I listened with a mixture of nervous excitement and blissful ignorance. We knew something important was happening, but we weren't quite sure what it was—or at least I wasn't. We kept peeking around the corner, and seeing how close we could get to the birth room before scurrying back to our parents' room and hiding under the covers. For once we had free rein to jump on their bed, but the allure of the events down the hall kept drawing us closer. Finally, Ruth was born and my dad brought out Baby Ruth candy bars to celebrate.

While that experience remains my first vivid memory, other childhood memories can be triggered through family photo albums or, a favorite pastime for many, slide shows. My family used to love setting up the slide projector and screen in our basement so we could view picture after picture capturing scenes from decades ago. For the pictures that predated my time, much of what I saw seemed completely foreign to me. Did my parents really dress like that in the 1970s? I had to see it to believe it. And the hairstyles?! Perhaps some things are best forgotten.

Remembering is a critical part of Communion—part, we should note, but by no means all of it. By God's grace the bread and cup become for us symbols that convey, far more powerfully than mere pictures ever could, a living reality that is Christ's presence with us. Photos and slides might aid our memories of key moments and events in our families' histories. In an even more wonderful way, the bread and cup of the Eucharist aid the church's memory, our memory of the story that defines us and makes us part of the family of God: the life, death, and resurrection of Jesus Christ.

Remember: It's the Lord's Supper

Still, sometimes we might have difficulty remembering something, even when it comes to the most important things. If we have ever struggled to remember and practice an integral element of our faith, like forgiveness, compassion, or reconciliation, then perhaps we can take some consolation in knowing that from the earliest days of the church, Christians have not always remembered well the good news of God's grace and acted accordingly.

The situation that the Apostle Paul addresses in 1 Corinthians 11 is in fact a major problem. The early Christians who were his original audience had not remembered rightly what the Lord's Supper was all about. Paul writes plainly, "Now in the following instructions I do not commend you, because when you come together it is not for the better but for the worse. For, to begin with, when you come together as a church, I hear that there are divisions among you; and to some extent I believe it" (1 Corinthians 11:17-18). As this passage indicates, division in the church is a problem that goes back to the earliest days of the Christian movement. Sadly, we see the effects of division today as well, and it is something that every congregation must be aware of and work hard to overcome.

Paul mentions that one way this division manifests itself is in a terrible abuse threatening the integrity and very core of their community. He asserts, "When you come together, it is not really to eat the Lord's supper. For when the time comes to eat, each of you goes ahead with your own supper, and one goes hungry and another becomes drunk" (1 Corinthians 11:20-21). When these early Christians came together, they thought they were celebrating the Lord's Supper, but it was really more like *their* supper rather than the Lord's—they were doing things their own way, not God's way. They had forgotten what God expected of them. They did not wait for one another. They did not share. Some remained hungry while others ate and drank so much that they were stuffed and even drunk.

Paul censures the people in strong terms: "What! Do you not have homes to eat and drink in? Or do you show contempt for the church of God and humiliate those who have nothing? What should I say to you? Should I commend you? In this matter I do not commend you!" (1 Corinthians 11:22).

> To live as God calls us to live, we must remember carefully. We must remember who God is, as Christ shows us; and we must remember who we are, and who we are called to be, in Christ.

Accurate remembering about what life with God entails, and specifically about the nature and purpose of Communion, is not a new challenge for the church. It is a challenge that Christians have faced from the beginning, and one that Christians have responded to sometimes well and other times poorly.

For us, today, to live as God calls us to live, we must remember carefully. We must remember, first of all, who God is, as Christ shows us; and we must remember who we are, and who we are called to be, in Christ. We all misremember occasionally, and the Eucharist is a wonderful way to re-remember Truth. Remembering is critical for us as God's people.

That is what Paul reminds us of in what he goes on to write:

> For I received from the Lord what I also handed on to you, that the Lord Jesus on the night when he was betrayed took a loaf of bread, and when he had given thanks, he broke it and said, "This is my body that is for you. Do this in remembrance of me." In the same way he took the cup also, after supper, saying, "This cup is the new covenant in my blood. Do this, as often as you drink it, in remembrance of me." For as often as you eat this bread and drink the cup, you proclaim the Lord's death until he comes. (1 Corinthians 11:23-26)

The message here applies no less in our time than it did so long ago. So much of what we need to remember as Christians is summarized in what Christ has said and done for us, specifically in the Lord's Supper. That, of all things, is essential for us to remember.

Remember: The Hope of Resurrection

One place that is meant to aid the human memory is a cemetery. A cemetery, of course, marks people's burial sites, often with dates, a symbol of some sort, or even a personal message, all designed to help us remember those who have gone before us. In one cemetery, a man's tombstone has a message inscribed with words from his wife who has outlived him. The message reads (in what seems to be unintentional humor), "My beloved husband, rest in peace...until I come."

After recalling the words of Jesus, Paul explains that "as often as you eat this bread and drink the cup, you proclaim the Lord's death *until he comes*" (1 Corinthians 11:26, emphasis added). This is a remarkable concept that we should not overlook. In the act of eating this bread and drinking this cup, we proclaim a new covenant that renders death meaningless in the resurrection power of Jesus Christ. This act makes a proclamation. This act sends a message. This act states what we declare in the Communion liturgy as we proclaim the mystery of our faith, "Christ has died. Christ is risen. Christ will come again."

The Lord's death is different than anyone else's death. It is different because, in Jesus, death is not the end. In Jesus, death does not have the final word. In Jesus, death itself dies because by his own death he defeats death. He deals death to death itself. Paul later taunts death and mocks it with these words: "Where, O death, is your victory? Where, O death, is your sting?" (1 Corinthians 15:55). Jesus promises that as it is for him, so shall it be for those who trust in him—the power of death is overcome.

When we come together for Communion, therefore, we do not simply look back to the past events of Christ's life and death the same way we might look back to the past events of someone else's life and death, like that of a family member or a friend. Communion is not simply about remembering "poor old Jesus" who was loved by many but died so long ago, never to be heard from again. That is not how it is! Yes, Jesus died, but he has been raised. Not even death has dominion over him. As he makes clear, "I am the first and the last, and the living one. I was dead, and see, I am alive for ever and ever; and I have the keys of Death and of Hades" (Revelation 1:17-18). Jesus also says, "I am the resurrection and the life. Those who believe in me, even though they die, will live, and everyone who lives and believes in me will never die" (John 11:25-26). In Jesus, death gives way to life, because in life and in death, he is the Lord, and we belong to him: "For to this end Christ died and lived again, so that he might be Lord of both the dead and the living" (Romans 14:9). In the face of human mortality, we can all find comfort in the resounding biblical affirmation of Christ's lordship and resurrection.

Remember: God Saves Us

Communion is an active recalling of Christ's final meal with his disciples. It is thus a life-affirming, life-imparting remembrance that draws us into the saving mystery of Christ. In Communion we remember what he has said and done for us not as mere past events, over and done with, but as completed actions that have enduring significance for us today and for all time.

Remembering in this way—as an active, living encounter with God—is represented especially in Holy Communion. Yet the principle is also found elsewhere, like in the Old Testament book of Joshua, and what we learn there can help us better remember God's presence with us today.

In Joshua 4, the people of Israel crossed the Jordan River. It was a milestone journey, promised by God, that had been literally generations in the making. Waiting all those years for the fulfillment of God's promise—that God would take the Israelites into the promised land—was a test of the people's collective memory, especially as they wandered for years in the wilderness.

Then finally, the moment arrived. When the people had finished crossing over the Jordan, God ordered Joshua to choose twelve Israelites, one from each tribe, and command them, "Take twelve stones from here out of the middle of the Jordan, from the place where the priests' feet stood, carry them over with you, and lay them down in the place where you camp tonight" (4:3). Joshua summoned the twelve Israelites and instructed them,

> Pass on before the ark of the LORD your God into the middle of the Jordan, and each of you take up a stone on his shoulder, one for each of the tribes of the Israelites, so that this may be a sign among you. When your children ask in time to come, "What do those stones mean to you?" then you shall tell them that the waters of the Jordan were cut off in front of the ark of the covenant of the LORD. When it crossed over the Jordan, the waters of the Jordan were cut off. So these stones shall be to the Israelites a memorial forever. (Joshua 4:5-7)

This momentous occasion became an exercise in remembering.

God told the people to take stones from the crossing of the Jordan River and to use those stones, down through the generations to come, as stones of remembrance. They were to be visible symbols of God's promises fulfilled. The stones were meant to help the people remember and trust in God once again. We would all do well to ask ourselves, "What stones of remembrance can I find in my life?"

Remember: God Promises a Hopeful Future

Pat Summitt retired in 2012 after thirty-eight record-setting years of coaching women's basketball at the University of Tennessee. During her tenure as coach, she won over one thousand games and eight national championships. Whether you like Tennessee orange or not (and my wife and her family, proud Kentucky fans, do not), there is no denying that she elevated the sport of women's college basketball and women's athletics in general. She wanted to keep coaching, but she retired because of early-onset Alzheimer's disease.

Summitt is widely known for her competitive spirit, which clearly comes across in her recent autobiography. At one point she claims, "What better way to kick a memory-wasting disease in the teeth—to keep my mind sharp and my heart engaged and my life in perspective—than with a memoir?" Her act of remembering was, on her part, a direct challenge to the exact condition that is diminishing her memory. In a lighthearted moment, she says that she sometimes forgets she has been diagnosed with dementia.[1]

Summitt closes her memoir by admitting there is a lot that she does not know or understand about what lies ahead. But as she deals with the new reality of life with Alzheimer's, she is certain of this: "God doesn't take things away to be cruel. He takes things away to make room for other things. He takes things away to lighten us. He takes things away so we can fly."[2] Even as her memory begins to fade, these indelible truths remain etched in her mind.

Because of what God has done for us in Jesus Christ, and because of what God has done in our own lives, we can trust in God, who promises that those who hope in the Lord shall renew their strength and soar on wings like eagles (Isaiah 40:31). That is what it means to remember with our faith—this dynamic remembering that is not just about some past events, but realizes the ongoing implications of those events and even ushers us here and now, by faith, into the presence of the living God who is our life, our joy, and our hope, always and forever more.

Remembering a Twofold Offering: Christ's and Ours

So far this chapter on remembering has dealt with how Communion involves an active remembrance of what Christ has said and done for us. That is a crucial part of the role of remembering in Communion. Yet this sacrament also involves remembering in another sense. To explore that other sense, we turn to the related and sometimes overlooked concept of offering—Christ's and ours.

Holy Communion is an offering in two ways. First and foremost, it consists in Christ's offering of himself to God. That was an offering he made freely, once and for all on the cross, for the salvation of the world. In a secondary sense, and this is where we are most deeply drawn into it, Communion also involves our offering, by faith, of ourselves to God, in union with Christ's sacrifice for us. Now, what does all that mean?

When I was growing up, one of my favorite places to be was Memorial Stadium in Baltimore to cheer for the Orioles. My family would often make the trip to watch the Orioles, even during the difficult seasons when wins were hard to come by (yes, Orioles fans know what it is like to suffer). Over a series of several seasons, we noticed a pattern: Whenever my older sister Emily went with us to see a game, Cal Ripken Jr. would hit a home run. That happened so many times in a row that it was extraordinary. We would say on our way to the stadium, "Since Emily has come along with us this time, Cal Ripken is going to hit a home run." Then he would do it! We called her his good luck charm.

In baseball, one person's act can have huge implications for the entire team. When someone hits a home run, the whole team benefits from that one person's action. There is only one person at bat at a time, so for a person to hit a home run, that person must do it alone, unaided by anyone else on the team. Yet there is a sense in which the entire team participates in that one player's action. The team benefits from that hit and the run or runs produced by it, and then the team further participates with that one player, and participates as a whole, toward the goal of winning the game.

Like every analogy, this one breaks down at some point. But it is one way for us to understand how the action of Christ, which he has done by himself, with no help from us, is not only something that we benefit from but also something that we, in turn, participate in as we move toward the goal of God's purposes for our lives and for this world. It is Christ's act that accomplishes so much for us—the salvation of our souls. Yet by God's grace, we come through our faith in Christ to participate in the outworking of the implications of that act in our lives. We come to participate by offering ourselves to God, in union with Christ's offering of himself for us.

Communion is about Christ's offering to God on our behalf as well as our offering of ourselves, in Christ, to God. Christ's offering to God for us is different than any other offering that has ever been made or could be made. In the Old Testament, there is a detailed sacrificial system that explains the different offerings the priests were to make to God on behalf of the people. That whole system of sacrifices foreshadowed the supreme offering to be made by Christ. The letter to the Hebrews tells us just how much greater Christ's offering is than any of the other offerings presented to God: "Every priest stands day after day at his service, offering again and again the same sacrifices that can never take away sins. But when Christ had offered for all time a single sacrifice for sins, 'he sat down at the right hand of God,' and since then has been waiting 'until his enemies would be made a footstool for his feet.' For by a single offering he has perfected for all time those who are sanctified" (Hebrews 10:11-14). No other offering could enable us to stand without blemish before God, but Jesus's single offering of himself can and does. The doctrine of the Trinity clarifies what is happening here: God does not send someone else to do the dirty work; rather, in Christ, the one true God has come among us as fully God and fully human, and Christ's sacrifice reveals the self-giving love of God that is truly redemptive.

Communion is about Christ's matchless offering for us all, his once-for-all sacrifice of himself to God on our behalf.

Holy Communion is also about our offering of ourselves to God, imperfections and all. We can offer ourselves to many different things. There are many gods vying for our attention and worship. For some people, it is the pursuit of these false gods that leads them to make offerings that should never be made.

This is not a new phenomenon. In the early church, Ananias and Sapphira sold a piece of property but kept back some of the proceeds for themselves while claiming to have given it all to the church. As Peter says to Ananias, "You did not lie to us but to God!" (Acts 5:4). Ananias and Sapphira ended up dying for a lie that they had given themselves to in the name of greed (see Acts 5:1-11).

There are many common idols across the generations, scores of alluring but ultimately unworthy recipients of human offerings. We hear about them practically every day in the news. In one flagrant example, the story broke in August of 2013 that the Assad regime in Syria used chemical weapons on their own people. Why? Presumably it was a show of the leader's power over against opposing voices. It was not just those actively resisting this regime who suffered, but also many innocent civilians, including children. Leaders killing their own people to extend their own pursuit of power—that is nothing new, but it is so tragic that with every example down through the ages we come face to face with our desperate need for a Savior. On our own, we are lost!

Closer to home, here in the United States idols abound. One of the biggest television events each year is the Super Bowl. In 2014, an audience of over 110 million people tuned in. As a big sports fan (admittedly verging on the idolatrous myself in that department), I was one of them. Much less coverage, in fact very little at all, focuses on the sex trafficking that goes on at the Super Bowl as well as other major sporting events, but tragically it is real. This sinister industry grosses almost $10 billion annually in the U.S. alone.[3] Young women, many of them children, are lured, taken, drugged, and, against their will, exploited for sex, all to satisfy the lust and greed of those who prey on them. Lives are shattered. The sex trafficking industry—a form of modern-day slavery—is a perverted, demonic representation of what many people in our society evidently value, pursue, and offer themselves to, at great harm for themselves and those affected. We need a Savior. On our own, we are lost!

We have been made to worship the one true God, in whose service is perfect freedom. Yet we often find ourselves enslaved, at least to some degree, and held captive in service to other gods. John Calvin candidly described the human heart as a perpetual idol-making factory. In myriad ways, human experience confirms that sobering observation. The results are detrimental on so many levels. Nevertheless, the redemptive message of the gospel is that Jesus came into this world—came to us—to set the captives free and proclaim God's favor (Luke 4:18-19).

In response to the human inclination for us to worship and give ourselves to false gods, I find it helpful to consider the response of the first disciples to the words of Christ. That is because in those first followers of Jesus we see glimpses of ourselves, in some cases positive and in other cases negative. After hearing Jesus say and do these extraordinary things, instituting the Lord's Supper through which mortal human beings commune with the immortal God, the disciples completely missed the point. They did not express, right then and there, their utter amazement at God's mercy and grace. Instead they began to argue among themselves as to which of them was the greatest (Luke 22:24-27)! They did not grasp at that moment that Christ was showing them a new and better way, the way of life, which is found not in vain, selfish pursuits, not in lording it over others and certainly not in harming others, but rather in self-giving service to the truth. The disciples were right there with Jesus, and yet they still did not get it. In many ways, we do not get it either.

We gather together in worship not because we are the righteous ones or those seen as great in the eyes of the world. We gather, instead, on every Lord's day, to recognize before almighty God our own brokenness. We gather before the Lord because we remember and give thanks to God that, in his infinite mercy, Christ was willing to be broken with us and for us. We come because in offering ourselves to God, in union with Christ's offering for us, as the Communion liturgy states, we can all find healing, wholeness, and renewed strength to serve God and our neighbors.[4] That is good news for a confused and hurting world, and yet a world so loved by God that God would give his only Son as an offering of mercy and grace for us all.

What that gift entails for us, God makes clear in these words from Scripture: "Therefore be imitators of God, as beloved children, and live in love, as Christ loved us and gave himself up for us, a fragrant offering and sacrifice to God" (Ephesians 5:1-2). Christ's loving, once-for-all gift of himself—in his life, teachings, suffering, death, and resurrection—demands from us a sacrifice of love in return, a sacrifice of ourselves, with nothing held back. The Eucharist is a sacrifice in a twofold sense, expressing both Christ's sacrifice of himself to the Father and our offering of ourselves, of all that we are, united with Christ's own sacrifice to God.

On March 24, 1980, Archbishop Oscar Romero, an outspoken critic of El Salvador's oppressive government, was killed in San Salvador while presiding at the Eucharist. In his sermons, which were broadcast by radio around the country, he had called on Salvadoran soldiers, as Christians, to obey God and had demanded an end to the repression. After finishing his sermon that day, he walked to the middle of the altar. Suddenly a shot rang out. According to an eye witness, Romero "held on to the cloth on the altar for a moment and pulled it off. Then he fell backwards and lay bleeding at the feet of Christ." An audio recording of the Mass indicates that Romero was shot while raising the chalice during the celebration of the Eucharist. For Romero, remembering the sacrifice of Christ also entailed literally the sacrifice of his own life.[5]

The sacrificial aspect of Communion may be relatively obscure, as it is often overshadowed by an emphasis on the memorial nature of the sacrament. But the idea of the Lord's Supper as a sacrifice holds crucial significance both theologically and practically in its call for us to offer our lives to God in and through Jesus Christ, who has given his life for the salvation of the world. That is part of what it means to remember rightly the presence of Jesus with us in Holy Communion.

Remembering the Call for Obedience

In his sermon "The Duty of Constant Communion," Wesley lists a number of benefits of communing with God "constantly," that is, as often as God gives us opportunity. They are benefits of what we might call remembering rightly, and so encountering afresh, the presence of the risen Christ in the Lord's Supper. Partaking in the Lord's Supper, done at the Lord's command, imparts to us the grace of God. In what are nearly Christ's dying words, he commands his disciples: "Do this in remembrance of me" (Luke 22:19). The benefits of receiving the sacrament, Wesley writes, "are so great to all that do it in obedience to [Christ]; namely, the forgiveness of our past sins and the present strengthening and refreshing of our souls." What God gives us here is "the food of our souls: this gives strength to perform our duty, and leads us on to perfection." While obeying Christ is its own reward, in addition to the joy of obedience, the Lord also conveys spiritual blessings to God's people through the Eucharist.[6]

Wesley spends the remainder of the sermon responding to some common objections against constantly receiving the Lord's Supper. It is remarkable how timely many of those objections remain. For instance, what pastor has not heard a version of this specious claim, "If we have Communion more often, it might not be as meaningful"? As in Wesley's day and time, still today there are challenges for us in the church to remember rightly and duly celebrate the presence of Christ among us. There are obstacles to "constant communion," or to receiving the Lord's Supper as often as possible. If we are not careful, problems like the following might prevent us and our congregations from experiencing the fullness of communion to which God calls us.

Call to Our Hearts and Minds

One of the chief obstacles to constant communion is mindless, heartless repetition. On one Sunday, as the pastor approached the pulpit to give the traditional call to prayer, he noticed that the microphone was not working properly. So he said, "There's something wrong with this microphone." The congregation promptly responded in rote fashion, "And also with you." It is possible not only for lay people but for pastors as well to check out mentally and spiritually during parts of worship. As a result, both laity and pastors may begin simply going through the motions in a kind of mindless and, worse, heartless repetition of the all-too-familiar words.

God spoke of this ancient problem through the prophet Isaiah: "These people draw near with their mouths and honor me with their lips, while their hearts are far from me, and their worship of me is a human commandment learned by rote" (29:13). Aware of this problem, Jesus himself quoted Isaiah in his condemnation of vain worship (Matthew 15:8). The words leading up to our reception of the Lord's Supper have tremendous significance. They retell decisive moments in salvation history, focusing especially on Christ our Savior and what he has done and said. Like any other part of worship, this part can become something we robotically repeat if we do not give it the attention it deserves or if we simply take for granted what is familiar. Conversely, by careful examination, not just of the words but particularly of our hearts and lives, we are able, through what is said and done in these holy moments, to prepare ourselves to meet the risen Lord in the Eucharist. Then our souls can be strengthened and refreshed as described by Wesley and, moreover, as promised by Christ.

Call to Be Present and Worship

Another hindrance to the kind of communion that God desires for us to experience is absence or neglect on the part of parishioners. While attendance in certain congregations increases on Communion Sundays, in other churches the opposite might be true. In such settings, at least some otherwise active churchgoers routinely skip worship when the Lord's Supper is celebrated, or perhaps leave worship right before communing, and they could do so for any number of reasons. One woman refuses to come because she dislikes the manner in which people receive Communion in her congregation. Rather than coming forward to the altar to receive, she favors reception in the pews; and she feels so strongly about it that she simply stays home and avoids Communion altogether when it is not done according to her preference. Some of the excuses for missing

Communion can be quite creative. Then, of course, there is the fairly standard time concern that with the Lord's Supper included in worship people might be late for dinner—*their* supper—at home or a local restaurant, or for a sporting event or some other apparently preferred activity. In any case, do people realize what they are missing? Wesley states plainly what is at stake:

> If . . . we have any regard for the plain command of Christ, if we desire the pardon of our sins, if we wish for strength to believe, to love and obey God, then we should neglect no opportunity of receiving the Lord's Supper. Then we must never turn our backs on the feast which our Lord has prepared for us. We must neglect no occasion which the good providence of God affords us for this purpose. This is the true rule—so often are we to receive as God gives us opportunity. Whoever therefore does not receive, but goes from the holy table when all things are prepared, either does not understand his duty or does not care for the dying command of his Saviour, the forgiveness of his sins, the strengthening of his soul, and the refreshing it with the hope of glory.[7]

Simply put, we neglect this gift of God's grace at our own peril.

To be sure, however, the responsibility does not fall solely to the people in our congregations. The church leadership also has a critical role to play. Whatever the state of a congregation's eucharistic life and overall spiritual vitality might be, the fact remains that pastors are called to lead. They are called by God to lead others, by precept and example, in the abundant life that Jesus came to give us all. Pastors should not only celebrate the Eucharist regularly but also teach about its importance. In churches that usually attract large crowds for Holy Communion, that promising attendance trend might signal a desire among many people in the church to learn more about Communion. Pastors and lay people alike can always benefit from gaining a greater understanding of this central aspect of our faith and all that it means.

For those churches that do tend to experience lower worship attendance or enthusiasm on Communion Sundays, that tendency can be viewed from several perspectives. Pastors for whom worship attendance statistics are an overriding concern could, I suppose, see this trend as a reason to celebrate the Eucharist less. But that would be a tragic mistake. The Lord's Supper is not the problem; on the contrary, it is a key solution to the real problem of spiritual apathy and slumber, and one of the greatest resources given to us by God. Other pastors might be less inclined to include the Eucharist in worship because it takes away precious time from the sermon. Would we rather hear ourselves preach than do as Christ commands? Sometimes the best thing for pastors to do is get out of the way and yield to God's work.

In America, United Methodists—like Christians from other traditions—face the challenge of resolving a problem deeply embedded in their own history. In early American Methodism, an ironic necessity left Wesley's followers confined to the practice of the Lord's Supper far less than every Lord's day as Wesley had promoted.[8] A shortage of pastors meant that pastors rotated among churches on the circuit. As a result, early American Methodists became accustomed to receiving Holy Communion only when the pastor was present. It is a paradox that heirs of Wesley, a proponent of constant communion, might really think that we are only supposed to celebrate the Lord's Supper on the first Sunday of the month and no more. Methodists can learn from other traditions where despite similar historical challenges more frequent eucharistic practice has taken hold, like Lutheran churches and Disciples of Christ churches, whose celebration of weekly Communion coincides with the practice of the early church.

No matter what the obstacles to constant communion may be in any given situation, Christ has power for us to overcome them. Because he does, we can learn to remember rightly that he gives himself to us in Holy Communion, which is a gift not to spurn but to receive joyfully, as intended, with open and thankful hearts.

A Desire to Remember

To be human is to long for community, for a place to belong and a connection to share with others. At its deepest level, this quest for communion is part of what it means that human beings have been created in the image of God. Because God, the Trinity, is the source of our life, relationship is at the heart of all reality. The explosive growth of social media serves as a manifestation of the basic human impulse and need for us to connect with others and to remember those connections even across cyberspace or time itself. In fact, in recent years, questions have emerged about the legality of maintaining the Facebook pages of deceased people as a way of remembering them.

We Are Not Alone

In the face of this profound desire to remember that we are not alone, that we are loved and can love others as we journey through life together, Christianity has something uniquely important to offer. What the gospel tells us finds elegant expression in Augustine's famous prayer: "You have made us for yourself, and our heart is restless until it rests in you."[9] In other words, God has created each of us to experience true community, connection, and fellowship with God and others. The longing of our hearts for meaning, relationship, and love finds fulfillment in Jesus Christ and in the union with God that Christ's coming into the world makes possible for us through the Holy Spirit.

Most people, whether Christian or not, hunger and thirst for deeper, more meaningful, and purpose-filled lives. God is calling us to go beyond thin, surface-level existence to penetrate the very depths of our Christian faith. In that journey, we will discover that there is healing for the pain and brokenness in our lives and in this world. That healing comes through the Lord, who has opened his heart to us and shows us that it is a heart of sacrificial, self-giving love. Amidst signs of a growing spiritual hunger in many congregations today—a longing for authentic discipleship—it is our great privilege and calling as Christians to recognize those desires and feed them by remembering the presence of Jesus among us.

We proclaim a message that points to the living Lord, through whom we are loved, forgiven, set free, and transformed and nurtured into fullness of life. What we have to offer is Christ, crucified and risen, God incarnate not simply two thousand years ago, but alive and with us even now. His communion with us is more than virtual; it is in person, in flesh and blood.

One couple in the church I serve has adapted the ancient practice of fasting in preparation to receive Communion. In their case, they have chosen to abstain not from food but from Internet usage (beyond work e-mail) and television for one day before worship. As a result of this spiritual discipline, the couple has grown closer not only to God but also to one another. They have become more self-aware about the amount of time they spend online and watching television, and they have begun to desire more and take greater delight in time spent together and with their children. The meaning of the Lord's Supper has been more deeply impressed upon their hearts and lives. The taste, both physically and spiritually, somehow seems sweeter due to the fast, as they experience a communion in person that is more authentic and fulfilling than the virtual connections available online through Facebook and other social media.

What might Wesley's notion of constant communion mean for us today? It is not a state of continuous contact with others over the Internet (though for some people in this rapidly advancing technological age, their phones and computers seem to serve as an extra appendage). It is, rather, a matter of enjoying to the fullest extent a vital, enduring bond with God. The reason we should gladly come to the Lord's table, at his invitation, as often as possible is because there that bond grows deeper.

The sacrament of the body and blood of Christ feeds our souls in a way that nothing else can. Shortly before the distribution of the elements, simple gestures remind us of the presence of God with us: the passing of the peace, and the pastor's pointing toward and then lifting up the bread and cup, those outward and visible signs of an inward and spiritual grace. This, above all, is how the church remembers that God is with us.

In Holy Communion, we remember Christ's sacrifice and offer ourselves to the Father as living sacrifices united in and with Christ's offering for us. In the process, we ourselves are "re-membered"— knit together as one body in the Holy Spirit. Communion makes us whole not simply on an individual level, but communally as well.

As we receive the sacrament of Christ's body and blood, God's Spirit brings us together and unites us, and the whole church, as one: "one with Christ, one with each other, and one in ministry to all the world, until Christ comes in final victory and we feast at his heavenly banquet."[10] As we will explore further in the next chapter, in this way we are spiritually nourished for ministry in Christ's name.

Questions for Reflection

1. What are some of your deepest and most powerful memories? How have those experiences stayed with you over the years?

2. How is memory significant for us as God's people? Why is it important for us to remember, and what specifically should we remember most?

3. In the Eucharist, we offer ourselves to the one true God. Paul writes, "I appeal to you...by the mercies of God, to present your bodies as a living sacrifice, holy and acceptable to God, which is your spiritual worship. Do not be conformed to this world, but be transformed by the renewing of your minds, so that you may discern what is the will of God—what is good and acceptable and perfect" (Romans 12:1-2). Are there things that hold you back from giving yourself fully to the Lord? How can you address those areas of life so that you can present yourself to God "as a living sacrifice" in the way that Paul urges us all to do?

4. Elsewhere, Paul writes, "For just as the body is one and has many members, and all the members of the body, though many, are one body, so it is with Christ.... Now you are the body of Christ and individually members of it" (1 Corinthians 12:12, 27). How is the body of Christ "re-membered" or brought back together in the practice of gathering for worship and especially in the Lord's Supper? What difference does it make that God calls us to come together in or-

der to remember Christ's presence with us? What difference does it make to you in your daily life that you are part of the community of God's people entrusted with remembering in this way?

5. The next time you receive the Lord's Supper, pay close attention to what happens. Listen carefully to the words that are spoken. Notice the gestures that the pastor uses. Think about the movements that are made—the coming forward to receive, or the distribution in your seats as God's grace comes to you, or the kneeling of hearts and perhaps bodies as well. Take a few moments now to go over in your own mind what happens in the celebration of the Eucharist, this meal of thanksgiving to God. In what ways does this part of worship draw you into the presence of God?

Lord, you are our dwelling place from generation to generation. We remember and give thanks for all that you have done, and especially for coming to be with us in Christ. As we recall with gratitude and amazement Christ's sacrifice for us, we offer ourselves to you as a living sacrifice. By your Spirit, help us remember rightly who you are and who we are in you, that we may live to the praise of your glory; through Jesus Christ. Amen.

Celebrating the Bread of Life Given for All

Then Jesus said to them, "Very truly, I tell you, it was not Moses who gave you the bread from heaven, but it is my Father who gives you the true bread from heaven. For the bread of God is that which comes down from heaven and gives life to the world." They said to him, "Sir, give us this bread always." Jesus said to them, "I am the bread of life. Whoever comes to me will never be hungry, and whoever believes in me will never be thirsty."

—John 6:32-35

So far in this book we have viewed Communion in its proper context in worship as a prayer. It is a prayer of thanksgiving for God's saving purposes for this world from the beginning, purposes ultimately revealed in and achieved by Jesus Christ. We have also explored how this sacrament involves remembering what Christ has said and done for us not simply as past events but as present realities. In that remembering of Christ's offering to God for us, Christ's body, the church, is itself "re-membered," or gathered together as one, as we offer ourselves to God, by faith and in union with Christ's sacrifice for us. Now we come to a related aspect of Holy Communion, namely, the sense in which it provides spiritual nourishment. Through the Eucharist, God feeds our souls as we celebrate the bread of life given for all.

Sharing in a Meal as Friends

Almost all of us have had the experience of being the recipient of a carefully prepared meal. Maybe you recall meals at your grandparents' house or your parents' house, or special meals somewhere else with family and friends, like on holidays. Who can pass up turkey at Thanksgiving? When I think about the idea of a carefully prepared meal, my mind goes back to when Molly (who is now my wife) and I had our first date. She cooked my favorite dish, lasagna. Later I learned that it was her first time using that lasagna recipe. Her mom and sister had strongly advised her that she either cook something she was familiar making or suggest we eat out instead. The stakes were high, but Molly made a delicious meal that we both enjoyed that night. Suffice it to say, she had me from the first bite. I liked her lasagna, but even more, I liked the cook and hostess herself. I wanted to get to know her better. Thankfully, the interest was mutual. Many meals ensued, but I will never forget that one!

> Through Communion, Christ, the host, reveals to us something important about himself; he reveals his heart, which allows us to know him better.

Holy Communion is a special meal. It is special because it communicates what is central to our faith. Through it Christ, the host, reveals to us something important about himself; he reveals his heart, which allows us to know him better. So why did Jesus institute the Lord's Supper? Why did he say of the bread, "Take, eat; this is my body" and of the cup, "Drink from it, all of you; for this is my blood of the covenant" (Matthew 26:26-28)?

There has been much speculation over the years as to the meaning of these words, and the reasons Jesus would say and do this. First, why? Perhaps the most compelling explanation that I have come across has to do with friendship. Thomas Aquinas, a thirteenth-century theologian, said that one of the intrinsic reasons behind the Lord's Supper is the love of friendship.[1] Friends want to be together.

Recently, Molly and our two-year-old daughter, Annie, had their toenails painted. They both chose pink, Annie's favorite color. Annie was endlessly fascinated with her newly painted toes. The next morning, while Molly was away playing tennis, Annie sat on the living room floor looking at her toes, touching them, and giggling. Suddenly she said to me, "Mommy's pink toes are at tennis." I replied, "Yes, that's right." Then she continued, earnestly: "Soon Mommy will come back with her pink toes to play with me and talk to me." There is something special about the power of the presence of loved ones with whom we can share life together.

Through the Lord's Supper we share life with our loving God. But as it is truly his supper, why would Jesus do this at all? Why would he give himself to us in this way? He could have just said, "I am going to die for you. I want you to remember what I have done for you, and that I am with you in spirit." But no! Jesus does not say that. He says more, much more, than that. He says what he says and does what he does because, astonishingly, he wants to be close to us and wants us to be close to him.

Friends desire to stay connected with one another. The remarkable popularity of social media is due in part to the fact that human beings are social creatures. It is amazing the extent to which we can connect with friends and the world around us over the Internet. Built into our DNA is a longing for relationship. We are created for friendship, and the love of friendship is a special love.

But here the Lord speaks of a friendship much deeper than anything we can experience online. Jesus says to his disciples, "I have called you friends" (John 15:15). The message in this case does not come over Facebook nor by e-mail from heaven, and not by phone or fax either. This message of friendship is embodied, incarnate. It comes in flesh and blood. Jesus has a message to deliver, and he delivers it in person. As he explains, "No one has greater love than this, to lay down one's life for one's friends. You are my friends if you do what I command you. I do not call you servants any longer, because the servant does not know what the master is doing; but I have called you friends, because I have made known to you everything that I have heard from my Father" (John 15:13-15). Jesus calls us—you and me—his friends.

In saying this, the Lord reveals a timeless truth about who he is and what he has done. Jesus does not come to us to weigh us down or hold us back; he comes to love us and save us from the things that weigh us down or hold us back. He is here, with us and for us, because he loves us with the love of friendship and wants to nourish us in that love. Out of love, Christ took on a true human body for our salvation. It is the unique feature of friendship to share life together with friends, and the Lord Jesus—our good God and Friend—promises us the irreplaceable gift of his presence to communicate God's love to us.

What, then, is the meaning of the words of Jesus about Communion? To answer that question we have to consider not just the passages describing what he did in the upper room, how he shared the Last Supper with the disciples—his final meal with them before he would suffer and die. There are also other passages in the Bible that refer to Communion, none more mysteriously grand, or frankly more stunning, than in John 6.

God Gives Life through Jesus

Notice the stark realism in the words of Jesus here, to indicate the extent of the feeding of our souls by his grace. Jesus declares, "I am the bread that came down from heaven" (John 6:41). The original audience began to grumble about Jesus because he said this. "They asked, 'Isn't this Jesus, Joseph's son, whose mother and father we know? How can he now say, "I have come down from heaven"?'" (John 6:42 CEB). One would expect that if Jesus was overstating his case, perhaps exaggerating for the sake of effect, then he would indicate as much when faced with such a skeptical reply.

But the Lord does not back away from this claim at all. Instead, he intensifies it: "Stop grumbling among yourselves," Jesus answered (John 6:43 NIV). "Very truly, I tell you, whoever believes has everlasting life. I am the bread of life. Your ancestors ate the manna in the wilderness, and they died. This is the bread that comes down from heaven, so that one may eat of it and not die. I am the living bread that came down from heaven. Whoever eats of this bread will live forever; and the bread that I will give for the life of the world is my flesh" (John 6:47-51).

The people listening to him argued among themselves and asked, "How can this man give us his flesh to eat?" In response, Jesus asserted even more forthrightly: "Very truly, I tell you, unless you eat the flesh of the Son of Man and drink his blood, you have no life in you. Those who eat my flesh and drink my blood have eternal life, and I will raise them up on the last day; for my flesh is true food and my blood is true drink. Those who eat my flesh and drink my blood abide in me, and I in them" (John 6:52-56). Christians have traditionally seen a direct link between this evocative language and the Lord's Supper, the sacrament of Christ's body and blood.

Only Jesus Really Satisfies

In Communion, God nourishes our souls with what can truly satisfy the hunger and thirst of the human heart. Jesus says, "I am the bread of life. Whoever comes to me will never go hungry, and whoever believes in me will never be thirsty" (John 6:35).

Hunger and thirst are a basic part of human life. If a baby is hungry, the baby cries. It is the baby's way of saying, "I'm ready to eat. Feed me!" As every parent learns, newborn babies need to eat every two to three hours—and sometimes that is still not enough! The experience of parenting sheds new light on the Apostle Peter's words: "Like a newborn baby, desire the pure milk of the word. Nourished by it, you will grow into salvation, since you have tasted that the Lord is good" (1 Peter 2:2-3 CEB). For those who can provide for themselves, when they become hungry or thirsty, the natural response is for them to get something to eat or drink. Without food or drink the hunger or thirst continues, and then there is a greater chance of crankiness, even for adults. We now have commercials that tell us, "You're not yourself when you are hungry." We all hunger and thirst.

> The Lord invites us to partake of the bread of life, to come to him and believe in him, through this meal of love that he has prepared for us.

Again, Jesus says, "I am the bread of life. Whoever comes to me will never go hungry, and whoever believes in me will never be thirsty" (John 6:35). The Lord invites us to partake of the bread of life, to come to him and believe in him, through this meal of love that he has prepared for us.

Over the years Christians have spent a great deal of time thinking about how this can be, how we actually encounter Christ in the Lord's Supper. Across Christian traditions there is widespread affirmation of the real presence of Christ—that Christ is truly present here in a special way to feed our souls. But often, theologians do not try to explain precisely how.

A hymn by Charles Wesley expresses the point well:

O the depth of love divine,
    The unfathomable grace!
Who shall say how bread and wine
    God into us conveys!
How the bread his flesh imparts,
    How the wine transmits his blood,
Fills his faithful people's hearts
    With all the life of God![2]

God's grace, given in this holy mystery, is sure and real, even if the exact manner is too wonderful for us to comprehend.

Jesus Shows Us God

But it all comes down to this: If we want to know who God is, we must look to Jesus. Jesus shows us who God is. Jesus shows us God's love for us. Jesus says, "I have called you friends" (John 15:15), and he is with us as he has promised to be. So we can receive his love and be strengthened in our souls by the bread of life.

In the fall of 2011, my mother-in-law, Lois, was diagnosed with an aggressive form of cancer. For about twenty months, her body responded remarkably well to the treatments. But in June of 2013, her condition took a turn for the worse. The doctors did not expect her to live beyond that month. Still, she continued fighting, and she showed tremendous strength, courage, and faith in so many ways. Lois would often say, "I'm so grateful for the love of family and friends. I'm so grateful for the care of the doctors and nurses. I'm so grateful." We all thanked God for the gift of her life, and for every additional day that she was given to live. September 6, 2013, was a special day; it was her birthday. It was a time to celebrate life and simply to be present with her.

Throughout those weeks and months, as her journey with cancer progressed, many of her friends expressed their love and support. A number of them did so not only through their prayers and with cards and messages (even a "Happy Birthday" rendition on YouTube by her junior high students), but through visits as well. Two weeks after her birthday that year, God called Lois home. Often, we think back to the times we spent with her, and especially to that last birthday she experienced here on earth, that final time for us to celebrate her birthday, and hence her life, with the blessing of her physical presence.

There is something powerful about our physical presence with one another. Think of the friendships that have sustained you over the years, particularly in the difficult times. Friends naturally desire to share life together with one another. So great is the power of presence that we grieve when we cannot be with our longed-for friends—either because they have died, or because they have moved too far away to share daily joys in a physical sense with us.

Jesus, our Lord and Friend, does not deprive us of his presence.

He is with us always, as he promised. He has promised to meet us in this meal of thanksgiving that is the Lord's Supper, so aptly named because he is the host who serves us a feast of love that he has prepared, and who shares with us in that feast. He does all this so we can receive here, at the altar of God's grace, the gift of himself with us and in us.

The Meal That Unites Christians

Even with Our Enemies

Lest we deceive ourselves, this same Jesus who fills our hearts and lives with joy calls all who follow him to a certain way of life, and that life includes difficult demands. Simply naming Jesus as Lord is not enough: "Not everyone who says to me, 'Lord, Lord,' will enter the kingdom of heaven, but only one who does the will of my Father in heaven" (Matthew 7:21). "Whoever does not carry the cross and follow me cannot be my disciple" (Luke 14:27). The way of following Jesus is the way of the cross, and so of radical love of God and neighbor. Such love extends even toward those we find, by our own strength, unlovable. As Jesus commands us, "Love your enemies and pray for those who persecute you" (Matthew 5:44). Yes, Jesus comes to us, but we have no control over what he commands and does, or what he requires from us. The terms for authentic Christian discipleship are Jesus's to define, not ours. He calls us, among other things, to make sacrifices for him, and to honor his presence even among and with those whom we do not like.

Harry Wiggett, an Anglican priest and prison chaplain, often visited Nelson Mandela and other political prisoners in Pollsmoor Prison to celebrate the Eucharist. Each time he did so, a prison guard had to be present, as Wiggett explains, "to keep an eye on me and to hear every word that I said, to be sure that I was not passing on or receiving any politically inflammatory messages."[3] On one occasion, when during the liturgy Wiggett reached the passing of the peace, Mandela interrupted him and requested that he stop. Mandela walked over to the guard on duty, Christo Brand. "Are you a Christian?" he asked Brand. "Yes," he replied. Mandela insisted, "Well then, you must take off your cap, and join us round this table. You cannot sit apart. This is holy communion, and we must share and receive it together."[4] The prison guard removed his cap, joined the circle, and received the sacrament with Mandela and the other prisoners.

Mandela's example shows concretely what the Eucharist entails. Brand, the prison guard, was a white Afrikaner and as such received all the political and economic benefits of apartheid. Mandela was a member of the exploited and oppressed majority. As a prison guard, Brand represented the coercive power of the state. Mandela was a political prisoner. The lines dividing them were clearly drawn. Moreover, in Brand's Dutch Reformed Church, blacks and whites were not permitted to worship together. Yet Mandela had him join the others in worship. For Brand, a white prison guard, to respond so naturally to the invitation of a black man, the prisoner, was, in Wiggett's words, "deeply moving."[5] This man was Mandela's jailor, yet most determinatively of all he was his brother in Christ.

For Mandela to invite that man, especially under those circumstances, to commune with him and others demonstrates the far-reaching implications of Holy Communion. It is, to be sure, not simply one's personal communion or fellowship with Christ. The communion realized in this sacrament is also communion with others in Christ's name. Communion is inherently communal. What is the nature of the communion that we share with others in Christ? How far does or should the invitation to the Lord's Supper extend?

Even with Other Traditions

These questions point to the problem of visible disunity within the broader Christian church. The fact that Christians across the full spectrum of church traditions cannot presently enjoy eucharistic fellowship—cannot share together in the sacrament of the body and blood of Christ—is a difficult and complex issue that obviously cannot be resolved here. But our current brokenness and divisions must be seen in the context of the mystery of God's kingdom as it is already present and not yet fully consummated. As the ecclesial sense of Holy Communion reminds us, both positively and negatively, God calls us to live in that tension as we look ahead and work toward what is to come.

The United Methodist practice of open Communion is, at its best, a response to the reality of not only our brokenness but also Christ's desire that we all be made one as he and the Father are one (John 17:21). This practice is generally understood to signify ecumenical openness, in the sense that it is appropriate for all who follow Christ to share in this meal together. As Mandela, a Methodist, asked his jailor, "Are you a Christian?" In response to the man's affirmative answer, Mandela invited him to come join him.[6]

Without a careful explanation and consistent application, though, the idea of open Communion can lead to confusion. I once heard a pastor state (in a bizarre misreading of Wesley), "Whether you are a Christian or not, and whether you are a follower of another religion or not, you are welcome to receive the Lord's Supper because John Wesley called this a converting ordinance." It is true that Wesley used that phrase, but Wesley's reference to the sacrament as a *"converting"* ordinance denotes conversion from one degree of faith in Christ to another, higher degree, not conversion from no faith to faith.[7] So, for pastors and others leading worship, the challenge is to convey an invitation to the Lord's Supper graciously and appropriately.

The Invitation Is from Christ

I have found that the words of invitation in the order of worship serve as a useful tool in this regard: "Christ our Lord invites to his table all who love him, who earnestly repent of their sin and seek to live in peace with one another. Therefore, let us confess our sin before God and one another."[8] The invitation is not ours, but Christ's. So we come not on our own terms, but on the terms of the one who proclaimed, "The time is fulfilled, and the kingdom of God has come near; repent, and believe in the good news" (Mark 1:14-15).

When the time comes in the service of Communion to distribute the elements, I use some variation of the following: "All who come by faith in response to Christ's invitation are welcome to receive this gift of God's grace, whether or not you are a member of this congregation. We are not baptized United Methodist; we are baptized Christian, and our baptism and faith in Christ that make us one. Christ invites you. Come, taste and see that the Lord is good." When people receive Communion who are not church members or who might not be baptized, the occasion provides pastors with an especially appropriate opportunity to visit with those people at some point after worship in order to inquire about their journey of faith and their response to Christ's call to follow him.

Freely Given, Humbly Received

It was in following up with one visitor that I began to learn of a beautiful story of grace and faith. This woman was raised in the Roman Catholic Church, which imparted to her a strong faith in God. But after enduring the pain of several difficult relationships and moving to a new community, she struggled to find a place where she felt like she belonged. A single mom, she has since found a church home for herself and her son in the congregation I serve. Through that renewed sense of community and family, they have both grown in their faith. She has retained from her upbringing a high view of the significance of Holy Communion. When she comes forward to receive the sacrament, I see in her a reverence and humble piety that exude gratitude and the power of God's grace. Recently I learned that she has Celiac disease. Her body cannot properly process foods containing gluten, like most breads. Even so, she savors the taste of bread. The only time she eats any bread is during Communion. It is something she anticipates and looks forward to, and even though we now offer gluten-free bread as well, she chooses to eat the "regular" bread. It is more than her body can handle, but she continues to receive it joyfully. Its sweetness leaves a distinctive taste in her mouth. Communion is a highlight for her not only physically but most of all spiritually.

For all of us, Christ's presence in the Eucharist is, in a real sense, more than we can handle—too much for us—and yet it is given freely for us and to us. Here, the human desire and craving for genuine fellowship and reconciled relationships with God and others is exceedingly met. In the Lord, who was willingly broken for us, we are made whole.

The Mystery of Faith: God Is Here

Even in the midst of our limitations, brokenness, and divisions, Jesus Christ is God with us, God right here and God right now. We encounter his living presence palpably in the bread of life and the cup of salvation, through the work of the Holy Spirit. It is here that we feast by faith upon the bread of life, upon Christ himself. In Holy Communion, this great mystery of our faith, God's life is given and shared, in a manner suited to our creaturely senses but wondrously beyond us still. More than anything else, that is a presence worth celebrating.

We get to know others over a meal. There is a social component to eating and drinking that is important. The term *companion* derives from the Latin words meaning "with bread." Christ gives us this meal, and gives himself to us in it, so that we would come to know him better, so that we would commune with him and with others in him.

Our Wednesday worship at Otterbein United Methodist Church of Spry is like a breath of fresh air in the middle of a busy week. The people gather, a small but congenial crowd, often just those dozen or so church women who are so faithful in prayer (I hope every congregation has them!), my family, and me. As we share in Christ's peace, the room is filled with the sound of remarks like these: "It's so good to see you." "I'm praying for you." "God bless you." Most fittingly of all, we hear and say to one another "The peace of Christ" as we embrace and hug. The ladies have formed a dinner group that meets before the service. The atmosphere of warmth, joy, and laughter carries on from their fellowship meal right into worship.

Making a Difference

Because of the spiritual sustenance that God gives us through Holy Communion, this weekly service has made a difference in the life of the church I serve. The congregation's growth over the last four years, basically doubling our worship attendance as of this writing, has not been the most numerically spectacular given the actual numbers involved. But it has been consistent and ongoing, fueled by a spiritual revitalization at the heart of which, I believe, is more frequent corporate prayer and Communion. God has used that feast of our faith to nourish us in Christ and to generate an increased desire for God that has spread throughout the life of the congregation.

The Meal That Celebrates God's World

As a formative act that makes us one with Christ and with one another in him, the Eucharist is also a celebration of God's world. Its significance encompasses divine-human relationships and extends to the created world itself, which also hungers for the fullness of God's redemption.

When I was growing up, there was nothing quite like a meal at my grandparents' house. I loved my grandma's food—home-cooked, healthy, flavorful, and washed down perfectly by a glass of her fresh-squeezed lemonade. We always ate well at grandma's house. The meals she made for us were a symbol of her love. Homegrown, home-prepared food and juice can give us a unique satisfaction. Such food and drink in some sense symbolize the goodness of this world.

Celebrating God's Goodness

That is so, in a way unlike any other, for the food and drink in the meal of Holy Communion. Here elements of the natural world are taken up in the saving mystery of God's purposes: with the blessing of God, bread and wine or juice become channels of God's grace. In that way bread, the result of grain grown in the ground, and this juice, a product of the vine, represent the healed relationship with the world into which we are to live in the ministry of reconciliation that God has given us. Holy Communion celebrates the goodness of God to and in the whole world. To a considerable extent, Communion includes and involves creation itself; the created order has a part to play in this cosmic tribute to God's redemptive love. God prepares a meal for us using the natural stuff of the world, but with God's blessings it serves a supernatural purpose, bringing us closer to God and to one another here, in and through God's good world.

Recalling Our Need for Goodness

According to the biblical narrative, there is an intentional structure to how God created the world. The creation account in Genesis 1 reveals that deep structure by three key principles that it lays out. The first is the image of God in which God has made us all, a remarkable gift granting us the capacity to know, love, and serve God (Genesis 1:26-27). The second is the blessing of God and corresponding call for appropriate stewardship of the world, or God's blessing and our responsibility (Genesis 1:28-29). A third idea presented there is the goodness of God's world: "God saw everything that he had made, and indeed, it was very good" (Genesis 1:31).

All three principles are seriously compromised by the problem of sin, our willful rejection of God and thus of the deep inner logic behind and structure of the world, and our abuse of creation that signifies that rejection. Genesis 3 describes the role of the natural world itself, represented by the tree and the apple. But instead of obeying God, Adam and Eve flagrantly disobey God. Their disobedience reveals critical truths about the human condition as a whole. We generally do not like when someone tells us what is off-limits. We would rather determine our own limits for ourselves. We would rather be our own gods.

When I was about eight years old, my dad and I were playing baseball at a church picnic. We went in search of a foul ball in the field where we were playing, and we came across a large pole with a sign on it that said in large letters, "DANGER! HIGH VOLTAGE. DO NOT TOUCH!" My dad said to me, "Don't touch that pole." Sure enough, the next thing I did was touch the pole. Fortunately I was not shocked, though my dad was—shocked not literally, but by my brazen disregard for his instructions as well as common sense. He exclaimed, "What did I just tell you?" Rebellious children hear commands but disobey.

In one way or another, we are all like that. God tells us to take care of this world in a way that reflects God's own dominion, shown through self-giving love and compassion, but we act like rebellious children when we refuse to obey and do just the opposite, when we exploit the world's resources and do not care for this world, and for one another, as we should. God's commandments are clear: "I am the LORD your God...you shall have no other gods before me" (Exodus 20:2-3). But like fools we willingly set up other gods and worship them. God commands us to love one another (for example, 1 John 4:7), but we routinely rebel against God's love and fail to love others as God intends for us to do.

The rest of the Bible demonstrates both the consequences of our sin and God's utter refusal to abandon us despite ourselves. Time after time, it shows the working out of God's purposes for bringing reconciliation and restoration to this world and to our hearts and lives. For instance, in Romans 8, Paul writes about the present sufferings and groaning for liberation, for us and creation as a whole: "We know that the whole creation has been groaning in labor pains until now; and not only the creation, but we ourselves, who have the first fruits of the Spirit, groan inwardly while we wait for adoption, the redemption of our bodies" (vv. 22-23). Even in the midst of our sin-sick world, Paul confidently lifts up God's promise of future glory.

That future, though, is not so far off as to have no bearing on the present. Already God has given us the first fruits of the Spirit. In 1 Corinthians 15:23, Paul names Christ as the first fruits through his death and resurrection. God gives us access, here and now, to Christ and to his resurrection power. God is bringing about a harvest of righteousness, a world transformed in the Lord Jesus, and the first fruits are already available for us to see and taste.

Recognizing the Proper Use of the World

Christ conveys his power to us by our faith and through the sacraments, as God uses the stuff of the world—water for baptism, bread and the fruit of the vine for Communion—to give us his grace. Baptism and Communion represent the proper use of the world, in obedience to God's commands rather than disobedience as in the fall. Baptism is a sign of how water should be used, according to

God's saving purposes, to cleanse and renew us through new birth into a living hope, and to make us part of Christ's body, the church. Communion signifies how bread and wine should be used, in accordance with God's saving purposes, to feed us with the bread of life and to quench our spiritual thirst.

Despite the mess we have made of this world in our failure to care for it as we should, and despite the mess we have made of our lives in our failure to love God and love others as we should, and how through those failures we inflict pain on one another, on ourselves, and even on the world around us, despite all of that, God's purposes will ultimately prevail. Those purposes are for our redemption and the redemption of this world that God so loves.

Celebrating God's Good Fruit

Christ has prepared a feast of love for us all. Through his death and resurrection, he invites us—you, me, and all people—to come and share in it. Jesus said, "I am the bread of life. Whoever comes to me will never be hungry, and whoever believes in me will never be thirsty" (John 6:35). This gospel feast is a cause for celebration, even as creation itself, God's creation, longs to be liberated from its bondage to decay and brought into the glorious freedom of the children of God. Holy Communion is a celebration of God's world and God's good and saving purposes even as we ourselves, who have the first fruits of the Spirit, groan inwardly as we wait eagerly for our adoption as daughters and sons, the redemption of our bodies. It is a celebration of God with us, Jesus Christ, the bread of life given for the life of the world.

Questions for Reflection

1. In your own family, what has been the significance of feasting at family gatherings? How does the act of eating together promote fellowship and community? How is that also true for us all in the Lord's Supper?

2. Jesus said, "When you are offering your gift at the altar, if you

remember that your brother or sister has something against you, leave your gift there before the altar and go; first be reconciled to your brother or sister, and then come and offer your gift" (Matthew 5:23-24). In communing with Christ, we also commune with others in Christ. Are there people you need to forgive or ask for forgiveness? In the midst of what seems like an increasingly fractured and polarized world, how can Christians model for the world true reconciliation? What spiritual resources does God offer us in the Lord's Supper to form, empower, and equip us for such work?

3. A hymn about the Eucharist speaks of coming "with joy to meet my Lord" in this sacrament.[9] What is your typical state of mind when you receive the Lord's Supper? Have you ever come "with joy"? What would it mean for you to do so?

4. Consider the role of the natural world in Holy Communion, as represented by the bread and the fruit of the vine. Does the Eucharist teach us anything about how we should care for the world, as in not simply other people in the world around us, but even the material world itself? How is our celebration of God with us in Holy Communion also a celebration of this world that God has made?

5. Throughout the course of this study, have you come to desire participating in Holy Communion more regularly? If so, in what ways? Share this news with your pastor or church worship committee. If you are a pastor, consider offering the Eucharist more regularly. What might it take for you to do that?

Eternal God, you have lovingly prepared a feast for us in Jesus Christ our Savior. Thank you for sending your Son into the world. Jesus, we praise you, the bread that came down from heaven. Holy Spirit, nourish us with the bread of life, that Christ may dwell in us and we may dwell in him by faith. Use us to spread the gospel, in word and deed, throughout your world; in the name of Jesus. Amen.

A Foretaste of the Heavenly Banquet

While they were eating, Jesus took a loaf of bread, and after blessing it he broke it, gave it to the disciples, and said, "Take, eat; this is my body." Then he took a cup, and after giving thanks he gave it to them, saying, "Drink from it, all of you; for this is my blood of the covenant, which is poured out for many for the forgiveness of sins. I tell you, I will never again drink of this fruit of the vine until that day when I drink it new with you in my Father's kingdom."

—Matthew 26:26-29

Up to this point, this book has explored the meaning of Holy Communion as a prayer of thanksgiving (chapter 1), an active re-membering of Christ's presence (chapter 2), and a celebration of the bread of life given for the world (chapter 3). Along the way, we have at different times focused on the past and present dimensions of this sacrament. There is also a third dimension, a third temporal reference, one that deals with the future. That future element con-tributes to a balanced perspective of not only what happens in Holy Communion but also what it demands from us, as we live into the kingdom of God that is, at once, already present and not yet fully revealed.

The Lord's Supper is not simply a matter of past and present—a memorial calling us to remember what Christ has done for us and a means of grace and spiritual sustenance in the present. It also points forward to what is to come. God gives us a foretaste of the heavenly banquet here and now in this sacred meal, an anticipation of God's promises ultimately fulfilled.

The tendency among many in the church today, particularly in many mainline settings, is to stress the memorial aspect of Holy Communion. Yet a bare memorialism reduces the meaning of the Lord's Supper to nothing more than a shallow reminiscence of past events. For that reason it is not in keeping with historic Christian teaching as handed down, for example, by John and Charles Wesley, who explicitly rejected that reductionist perspective in their *Hymns on the Lord's Supper.*[1] Some people in the pews see beyond bare memorialism and happily realize the present effects of the sacrament. Comparatively rare, however, is the understanding especially among lay people that unites past, present, and future into an integrated whole. A vigorous, future-oriented sense of Holy Communion allows for such a balanced and holistic view because in the Eucharist the future breaks into the present and also brings to our minds the past. Without that third temporal component, which gives us a foretaste of what is to come, our understanding and practice of Communion would be cut short. But with it they can be greatly enhanced, in light of God's promised new creation where we will share fully in this feast of our faith with Christ and with all God's people. The Eucharist is a matter of not just remembering and celebrating Christ's presence, but also anticipating what is yet to come.

Anticipating the Heavenly Banquet

Babette's Feast is a movie about a lavish meal prepared by the refugee turned housekeeper Babette as an outpouring of her appreciation for the two sisters who take her in. After Babette wins the lottery, rather than spend the money on herself, she decides to cook a delicious, exotic dinner for the sisters and their small congregation on the occasion of the founding pastor's hundredth birthday. She never tells anyone that she has spent her entire winnings on the ingredients for this feast. Throughout the movie, anticipation builds about Babette's plans for this specially prepared meal, even among villagers who cannot help but wonder what is in store with the arrival of ingredients that they have never seen before. When the food is finally served, the film, which previously showed mainly white and gray, adds more colors with each delightful and delectable dish. The meal ends up being more wonderful than any of the recipients imagined, feeding both the body and the soul, elevating the human spirit, and even reaching a kind of mystical aura. It is, indeed, a feast to anticipate and savor.

The prophet Isaiah communicates a bold vision of God's promises fulfilled, and uses the language of feasting to describe that glorious day: "On this mountain the LORD Almighty will prepare a feast of rich food for all peoples, a banquet of aged wine—the best of meats and the finest of wines." With such plentiful, sumptuous fare, this is going to be the banquet of banquets. It will be a celebration of reconciliation and the defeat of death itself at the hands of God, as Isaiah continues: "On this mountain he will destroy the shroud that enfolds all peoples, the sheet that covers all nations; he will swallow up death forever. The Sovereign LORD will wipe away the tears from all faces; he will remove his people's disgrace from all the earth. The LORD has spoken." Isaiah's message of promised redemption ultimately comes not from a mere mortal, but from God. "In that day they will say, 'Surely this is our God; we trusted in him, and he saved us. This is the LORD, we trusted in him; let us rejoice and be glad in his salvation'" (Isaiah 25:6-9 NIV). To be sure, this is a feast worth preparing for and heartily anticipating.

Jesus spoke of the kingdom of heaven as a coming banquet, where there will be feasting. Once he told this parable:

> A certain man was preparing a great banquet and invited many guests. At the time of the banquet he sent his servant to tell those who had been invited, "Come, for everything is now ready."
>
> But they all alike began to make excuses. The first said, "I have just bought a field, and I must go and see it. Please excuse me."
>
> Another said, "I have just bought five yoke of oxen, and I'm on my way to try them out. Please excuse me."

Still another said, "I just got married, so I can't come."

The servant came back and reported this to his master. Then the owner of the house became angry and ordered his servant, "Go out quickly into the streets and alleys of the town and bring in the poor, the crippled, the blind and the lame."

"Sir," the servant said, "what you ordered has been done, but there is still room."

Then the master told his servant, "Go out to the roads and country lanes and compel them to come in, so that my house will be full. I tell you, not one of those who were invited will get a taste of my banquet." (Luke 14:16-24 NIV)

According to Jesus, none of those invited who refuses to come will end up getting a taste of this great dinner. When our Lord likens the kingdom of heaven to a banquet, the implication is that we, as his servants, should go out and bring in the poor, the crippled, the blind, and the lame. In other words, Jesus basically commands us, "Go out and bring in the people no one else sees or wants, because I want them to come to my banquet." I love that about Jesus.

Anticipating Our Own Invitation

When our eyes and hearts are opened by God's grace, we can see glimpses of the banquet described by Jesus in all its extraordinary expansiveness and surprising, challenging, and abiding concern for those so often overlooked or forgotten. In 2005, when I was a student at Duke Divinity School, I spent five days over spring break living in a L'Arche community in Ontario, Canada. It is part of a global network of hundreds of places where people with special needs and their caregivers live together in Christian community. L'Arche communities take their name from the French word meaning "the ark." It is a reference to the familiar Bible story because, just like the animals on Noah's Ark, everyone has a place there. At L'Arche, outcasts of society are welcomed into God's ark. These people Jesus deeply loves find not only a place at the dinner table but also in fact a home. During my time in Ontario, I witnessed love in action in ways that were truly uncommon. It did not matter that three of the five residents in the house where I stayed could not even speak. They used other means of communication, like gestures and grunts, and in their own way they made it clear, from the start, that my friends from Duke and I were welcome among them.

We had come from a major research university, a place of educational renown, but I learned more from the L'Arche community than I ever could have learned from a lecture or class assignment. The people in that place taught us about the rich feast of life together in Christ. They modeled it for us, with the lighthearted teasing at the dinner table; the group prayers several times throughout the day; the simplicity and joy; and the compassion of the caregivers, who literally bathed the residents who could not bathe themselves.

Hanging on the walls in the home where I stayed were two reminders of the calling that we all have to love others as the friends of Christ. One was a placard with a quotation from 1 Peter 4: "Above all, maintain constant love for one another....Like good stewards of the manifold grace of God, serve one another with whatever gift each of you has received" (4:8, 10). The people of that community lived those words.

The other reminder of the love of God that I saw spoke even more powerfully: an icon of Christ on the cross, his hands gracefully outstretched as if to reach the whole world. After seeing this icon, I thought to myself, "No wonder such embracing love is manifest here. Christ is here, and these are his friends, living in him, loving one another in him." My time at the L'Arche community was a foretaste of the anticipated banquet.

Just as Christ was there, in that place, so he is with us wherever we may be. He is saying to each of us, "Come and live in me. I will give you abundant life." He will open our eyes so we can see the world in the light of his grace, so we can look around and ahead in trusting anticipation of God's new creation.

God gives us a foretaste of the heavenly banquet here and now in Holy Communion.

God gives us a foretaste of the heavenly banquet here and now in Holy Communion. Matthew 26 teaches us that Jesus will share in this meal with us in heaven. Jesus says, "I will never again drink of the fruit of this vine until that day when I drink it new with you in my Father's kingdom" (Matthew 26:29). In Communion we anticipate what is to come. We are given a foretaste of God's promises fulfilled.

Anticipating Great Reunion

What do we anticipate in life? What do you anticipate and look forward to today? It could be any number of things. Perhaps you look forward to a promotion at work, a child's graduation, an anniversary, or simply retirement. Most of us anticipate a certain stage of life or position. Hopefully, at a very deep level we all anticipate that great reunion with loved ones in the kingdom of God.

Anticipating Promises and Dreams Fulfilled

Anticipation has always been important for God's people. For example, consider once more the story of Joshua leading the people into the promised land (Joshua 1–4). It was the fulfillment of a promise God had made generations before. The people had to step out in faith, to anticipate what God would do, and actively prepare as God would lead them. They needed faith and courage as they trusted in God. They needed faith and courage as they actively anticipated God's promises fulfilled.

One common practice when a church gets a new pastor is for that congregation to hold a series of home gatherings. The purpose of those meetings is to give people from the church a chance to get to know the new pastor and vice versa, and to give them all a chance to talk as a group about the church—past, present, and future.

Every once in a while, often several times per year, I will review my notes from such meetings, especially out of interest in reading again what people said about their hopes and dreams for the congregation. A number of the comments from people in my current setting hit on common themes, such as these: "We want our church to be a vital, growing church that reaches out into the community, connects with people, invites them to our church, and welcomes them when they come." Others put it this way: "Our hopes and dreams are for this to be a more active church, to start a new worship service, and to bring more people of all ages, especially children, youth, and young families, into the embrace of our loving church family. Our hopes and dreams for this church are for God to grow our ministries across the board so we can share the good news of Jesus with more people." When pastors hear comments like that, they are usually inspired.

I suspect that most congregations have at least some people who would express aspirations like these if given the opportunity. It can be a useful exercise for pastors and lay people to discuss such ideas. I have had the privilege of serving a church where a lot of people dare to believe God's promises, confidently claim them, and dream big dreams, God-sized dreams. It has been exciting to watch how the Lord has made many of those dreams a reality.

Wherever you may be, either individually or in the congregation you attend or serve, you can be certain of this: God is calling you forward. God has brought you along the journey, and the next step is now before you. What does that next step look like for you or for your congregation? Where is God calling you to go and what God is calling you to do? What is God calling you to anticipate as you seek to grow in Christ and in ministry in his name?

As individuals and congregations follow where God leads, amazing things await. Drawing from Isaiah 64:4, Paul writes that "no eye has seen, nor ear heard, nor the human heart conceived, what God has prepared for those who love him" (1 Corinthians 2:9). As you claim God's promise of a future with hope, you can expect God to be at work. You can expect to see resurrection power!

One Epiphany tradition involves baking a ring or figurine inside bread or cake. The ring or figurine represents Jesus our King. Predictably, when the time comes to eat this treat, there is a sense of anticipation about who will get the special piece. People bite into the bread or cake carefully so they do not damage a tooth or shift any dentures.

Jesus is in the bread of Holy Communion for us all; it is the sacrament of his body, and through it we all receive his presence by faith. Here and now we receive a foretaste of God's promises fulfilled. Here and now we anticipate the heavenly banquet where we will feast forever with Jesus and with those we love. One of the chief tasks of the church is to bring as many people with us to that banquet as we can.

Bringing People to the Banquet

For our salvation, Jesus took up the cross in self-giving service to the world. The cross is integral not only to our faith overall but also to the Eucharist in particular. Moreover, Jesus spoke repeatedly about the cost of following him in words like these: "If any want to become my followers, let them deny themselves and take up their cross daily and follow me. For those who want to save their life will lose it, and those who lose their life for my sake will save it" (Luke 9:23-24). As a profound experience of unity with Christ and with others in Christ, Holy Communion constitutes, for us all, a radical call to serve Christ and this world by giving of ourselves, taking up our cross, and following him.

With Joy and Delight

Our two-year-old daughter, Annie, gets so excited about the Lord's Supper that sometimes I have to hold her back from the bread and cup because it is not yet time. Then after worship ends, she squeaks in her little voice, "More, please!" She eats "the yummy Jesus bread," as she calls it, like we have not fed her all day. It is fun for us all to watch as she anticipates and then delights in this great feast of our faith. For her, one little piece is not enough; it only seems to make her hungry for more.

In our setting, God has used that midweek service to arouse a spiritual hunger in our midst and to make our church more alive in various ways. It has since led to a full slate of Wednesday activities including a common meal and Christian education experiences for all ages. We see fruit in deepening friendships within the church, faith formation, and increased emphasis on prayer and the Eucharist. We also see fruit in new ministries to the community as well as renewed growth in some of our congregation's existing ministries.

For instance, I do not consider it a coincidence that two of the people who regularly attend the Wednesday prayer service approached me several months after we had begun the service and shared with me their sense that, following Christ's call for us to serve, our church should increase our efforts in feeding the hungry of our community. Out of those conversations there has emerged a new food ministry that supplements our weekly food bank and monthly food program. About once a quarter, we feed hungry people in the city of York. Between acquiring food donations, cooking, bagging, delivering, and cleaning up, it is a church-wide effort involving adults, youth, and even children. One of my favorite stories about these various feeding ministries has to do with a nine-year-old girl from the congregation. She asked all the people who were coming to her birthday party to bring canned goods instead of traditional gifts; she, in turn, donated all those canned goods to the church food bank, which serves the community.

With Greater Love

The congregation, while not particularly large, has become increasingly mission-minded. We have found what seems to be our missional niche through serving others with food as an expression of Christ's love. In all, most of our active worshipers support our food ministries in some way, and the church now feeds dozens of families each week and thousands of people over the course of the year.

As we serve we try to build deeper relationships with the people we have come to know through our outreach to the community, and to invite them into the life of our church. We want to bring them to the banquet of God's kingdom. That relational approach to evangelism has yielded positive results in this setting, as numerous people have become part of our church family through our feeding ministries to the wider community. In one way or another it all points back to the Wednesday prayer service and the simple act of gathering together weekly to open ourselves to the presence and power of the God who feeds us all. Our sharing in Communion has brought others to the banquet.

With Clearer Vision

In suggesting that we give proper attention to the sacraments as practices that increase spiritual and congregational vitality, however, I am not talking about trying to save a denomination. I do not know what, in the providence of God, the future of this or any other church tradition might be. Instead of mere denominational preservation, what I am talking about is a goal that is far greater and, in my opinion, more important: a dynamic movement of the Holy Spirit making more and more people, both individually and collectively, alive in Christ and growing into his likeness through the love of God and neighbor. When it comes to the Lord's Supper in particular, Christians have historically found in this gift a vibrant, formative encounter with Jesus Christ, crucified and risen, and a powerful means of grace.[2] The primary argument of this book has been that a deeper appreciation of the nature and purpose of Holy Communion can provide insights for giving this sacrament a more prominent role, not just in church life, but in the Christian formation of individuals today.

Take, Eat, and Drink: A Life-Imparting Banquet

One of those insights represents a culmination of all that has led to this point. The Eucharist not only contains within it various senses that contribute to its meaning, such as the ideas of remembering, celebrating, and anticipating; it also includes the corresponding temporal dimensions of past, present, and future. Furthermore, because we are physical beings we experience life through the senses, which makes it fitting for any communication that God shares with us to come through our senses. Holy Communion is a matter of all five senses, through which the Holy Spirit enables us to experience God's presence and power. This gift of God's grace engages the full range of human senses. Drawing us into a participation in the life of God, it deepens our faith and enhances our lives. It refreshes our souls and awakens us to true community in God's kingdom. Through Holy Communion, Christ imparts life to us—his own life, given for our salvation. With all its sensuous breadth and depth, this paradigmatic meal of our faith enables us to hear, see, smell, touch, and taste the abundance of God's goodness.

> This gift of God's grace engages the full range of human senses.

Answering the Call to Mission

Bobby is an evangelist. He cannot speak, but he is still an evangelist. A longtime member of the church I serve, Bobby recently moved to an assisted living facility for people with special needs. It is a wonderful community of people, and he has made good friends there. Although the drive lasts over thirty minutes one way (plus the time it takes to load up the special wheelchair-accessible van), Bobby still comes to our church. He not only comes but also brings his friends with him, sometimes as many as five other residents plus their assistants.

Bobby's friends have added much to our church's worship of God, including a sense that one never knows what might happen next. Sometimes—right in the middle of worship—one or several of them will suddenly erupt with laughter. One Sunday, while I was announcing the upcoming Easter program and egg hunt for the children of the church and community, one person from this group, James, stood up and shouted enthusiastically. Surprised to hear a sound like that coming from the congregation, I could not understand what he shouted. Yet it was loud enough to reverberate throughout the sanctuary, and too loud, I thought, to ignore. So I quickly said, "That's right. We can get excited about this event for our community!"

Being Open to What God Is Doing

A few months ago during Communion, something happened involving Bobby and his friends that, whether deliberately or not, bore witness to a deep spiritual truth. I had just invited the people to come forward at the direction of the ushers and to "taste and see that the LORD is good" (Psalm 34:8). All of a sudden, before the ushers could signal to him or to anyone else for that matter, James leapt up and took off; he darted right for the Communion station. His arms reaching, his hands excitedly held out, he was so eager to receive Communion that he did not wait, not even for the direction of the ushers! Or perhaps he was simply extremely hungry. Either way, something was happening at that moment that was not in the bulletin, something that was not in the pastor's master plan for worship, something that was not expected by anyone, least of all me. James even caught his assistant off guard, but once she realized what he was doing she immediately ran after him. He was too fast for her, though, and by the time she reached him he was already at the Communion station, literally groaning and panting as he stretched out his hands for the consecrated bread, as if this was precisely the moment he had been waiting for, as if his very life depended on it. Later, one person said to me, "Shouldn't we all be that excited to receive Communion?"

We are physical beings. We experience life through our senses. So if God is going to communicate with us, it would make sense for God to do so through our senses. Holy Communion is a matter of all five senses, through which the Holy Spirit enables us to experience God's presence and power. In this special means of grace, God reaches us through the full capacity of our senses. We hear Christ's words to us, inviting us to come to him. We see the bread and cup, profound symbols of God's love. We smell the aroma of God's grace as we approach the bread and cup. We touch—for ourselves!—the sacrament of Christ's body and blood, given freely for us all. Finally, we taste its earthy richness: the blessed bread, though materially less than the smallest of snacks, is still more than enough to satisfy the hungry soul; and the consecrated cup may be just a matter of drops, yet it mysteriously quenches our spiritual thirst. In these holy moments, and through faith, as a kind of sixth sense, the Spirit of God brings our senses themselves to a pinnacle too sublime for words.[3]

Drawing us into a participation in the life of God, Communion becomes the most grace-filled meal of all, deepening our faith and enhancing our lives.

Drawing us into a participation in the life of God, the most grace-filled meal of all deepens our faith and enhances our lives. In a way unlike anything else, through the life-imparting gift of Holy Communion—which is at once a prayer of thanksgiving, a remembrance of the Last Supper, an offering to God, a feasting on the bread of life, a communion with Christ and others, a celebration of God's world, a foretaste of the heavenly banquet, a call to service, and so much more, all to the glory of God—we hear, see, smell, touch, and taste the goodness of God. Simply put, through the work of God's Spirit in Holy Communion we celebrate the presence of Jesus Christ, God with us.

Questions for Reflection

1. There is a mysterious quality about the future because it is always beyond us, in one sense not yet fulfilled. As you look ahead, what do you anticipate about the future? What concerns or fears do you have? Do you think that in the midst of the inevitable uncertainty regarding various aspects of our future, there is still reason to be hopeful about what lies ahead for you, for your family, or for others? Why or why not?

2. Jesus describes the kingdom of heaven as a banquet in Luke 14:16-24. How does Holy Communion give us a foretaste of that banquet? In Matthew 26:26-29, Jesus promises his

disciples that he will "drink of the fruit of the vine" with them in his Father's kingdom (26:29). What does this idea—of not simply being fully in the presence of Jesus, but also having him eat and drink anew with us—suggest to you about the extent of fellowship with God that awaits us? Have you ever thought much about heaven as a feast with both God's people and also with Jesus himself? What images come to your mind as you envision that feast?

3. Of the three temporal senses of the Eucharist (past, present, and future), in which one or ones do you find the greatest meaning? Why?

4. The Eucharist engages all five human senses. Which of these senses seems most prominent or poignant to you as you participate in the Lord's Supper? Why?

5. Jesus said, "I am the bread of life. Whoever comes to me will never be hungry, and whoever believes in me will never be thirsty" (John 6:35). Commit those words of Christ to memory. Will you come to him as he graciously invites you? Will you, at this moment, believe and trust in the one who is the "joy of every longing heart"?[4] Will you commit yourself, or perhaps recommit yourself, to serving Christ and serving others in his name? What steps do you think God might be calling you to take in response to Christ's claim upon your life?

Gracious God, our Father in heaven, thank you for coming to us in Jesus Christ. Thank you, Jesus, for inviting us to experience your presence in the gift of Holy Communion. Holy Spirit, fill us with the life of God here and now. Open our eyes, God, to see your glory, our ears to hear your voice, our hearts to receive your love, our mouths to speak your praise, and our hands to do your work in this world; through our Lord Jesus Christ, who is Emmanuel, God with us, now and always. Amen.

Midweek Worship

Below is the order of worship used at the midweek service at
Otterbein United Methodist Church of Spry in York, Pennsylvania.
This order is based on an order of worship sent to me in 2010 by the
Reverend A. J. Thomas. It is my hope that other church leaders will
use or adapt it as they see fit.

An Order for Midweek Worship with Holy Communion

The people gather in silent prayer and reflection.
PROCLAMATION OF THE LIGHT
Leader: Light and peace in Jesus Christ.
People: **Thanks be to God.**
EVENING HYMN
To be chosen by the people or by the pastor.
SCRIPTURE READING
The main scripture reading for the upcoming Sunday is read.
A brief silence is kept for reflection.
AFFIRMATION OF FAITH
The Nicene Creed   *The United Methodist Hymnal,* 880
PRAYERS OF THE PEOPLE   *UMH,* 879
After each prayer, the leader concludes, "Lord, in your mercy," *and
all may respond,* **"Hear our prayer."**
     "Together, let us pray for
        the people of this congregation...
        those who suffer and those in trouble...

the concerns of this local community...
the world, its peoples, and its leaders...
the church universal—its leaders, its members, and its
mission...
the communion of saints...."

THE LORD'S PRAYER
INVITATION TO THE SACRAMENT OF HOLY COMMUNION
CONFESSION AND PARDON

Have mercy upon us, O God, according to your loving-kindness. According to the multitude of your tender mercies, blot out our transgressions. Wash us thoroughly from our iniquities, and cleanse us from our sins. Create in us clean hearts, O God, and renew a right spirit within us; through Jesus Christ our Lord.

All pray prayers of silent confession.

Leader: Hear the good news: Christ died for us while we were yet sinners; that proves God's love toward us. In the name of Jesus Christ, you are forgiven!

People: **In the name of Jesus Christ, you are forgiven! Glory to God. Amen.**

All greet each other with signs of reconciliation and peace.

THE GREAT THANKSGIVING

Leader: The Lord be with you.

People: **And also with you.**

Leader: Lift up your hearts.

People: **We lift them up to the Lord.**

Leader: Let us give thanks to the Lord our God.

People: **It is right to give our thanks and praise.**

The pastor gives thanks appropriate to the occasion, remembering God's acts of salvation, and concludes:

And so, with your people on earth and all the company of heaven we praise your name and join their unending hymn:

Holy, holy, holy Lord, God of power and might. Heaven and earth are full of your glory. Hosanna in the highest. Blessed is he who comes in the name of the Lord. Hosanna in the highest.

The pastor continues the thanksgiving. The institution of the Lord's Supper is recalled. The pastor concludes:

And so, in remembrance of these your mighty acts in Jesus Christ, we offer ourselves in praise and thanksgiving as a holy and living sacrifice, in union with Christ's offering for us, as we proclaim the mystery of faith:

Christ has died; Christ is risen; Christ will come again!

The pastor invokes the Holy Spirit, praises the Trinity, and concludes:

All honor and glory is yours, almighty Father, now and forever. **Amen.**

GIVING THE BREAD AND CUP

PRAYER OF THANKSGIVING

O Lord our God, your Word and your sacrament give us food and life. May this gift of your Son lead us to share his life always. We pray this in Jesus's name. Amen.

PRAYER SONG

"Jesus, Remember Me"   *UMH*, 488

DISMISSAL WITH BLESSING

Leader: The grace of Jesus Christ enfold you this night. Go in peace.

People: **Thanks be to God.**

Notes

Introduction

1. The other two chief means of grace according to Wesley are prayer, both corporate and private, and reading Scripture. For more, see Wesley's sermon "The Means of Grace." Wesley's sermons are included in volumes 1 to 4 of *The Bicentennial Edition of the Works of John Wesley* (Nashville: Abingdon Press, 1984–); henceforth referred to as Wesley, *Works*. Wesley's sermons can also be found online at: http://www.umcmission.org/Find -Resources/John-Wesley-Sermons.

1. A Prayer of Thanksgiving

1. The Articles of Religion of The Methodist Church, a. XVI—Of the Sacraments; and The Confession of Faith of The Evangelical United Brethren Church, a. VI—The Sacraments. As two of the doctrinal standards in The United Methodist Church, these sources can be found in *The Book of Discipline of The United Methodist Church—2012* (Nashville: The United Methodist Publishing House, 2012), ¶104.

2. Hugh of St. Victor, *De sacramentis*, IX, 2.

3. Augustine, *Confessions*, translated with an Introduction and Notes by Henry Chadwick (New York: Oxford University Press, 1992), VIII, 152–3.

4. Ibid., 153.

5. John Wesley, Sermon 16 (1746), "The Means of Grace," II.1, in Wesley, *Works*, 1:381.

6. For more, read Bonhoeffer's classic work, *The Cost of Discipleship* (New York: Macmillan Publishing, 1949).

7. Wesley, "The Means of Grace," II.1, in Wesley, *Works*, 1:381.

8. For more on Calvin's doctrine of the Lord's Supper, see Brian A. Gerrish, *Grace and Gratitude: The Eucharistic Theology of John Calvin* (Minneapolis: Fortress Press, 1993).

9. In what follows, I am drawing from the order of worship in *The United Methodist Hymnal* (Nashville: Abingdon Press, 1989), "A Service of Word and Table I," 7–11. Of course, resources from other church traditions also have much to offer. This particular order of worship, while endorsed by The UMC, reflects broad ecumenical consensus and commitments in addressing key themes related to Holy Communion. I use it here for that reason, and also because it is the order of worship for the Lord's Supper that I know best and the one that I have seen God use to revitalize the congregation I serve.

10. "A Service of Word and Table I," *The United Methodist Hymnal*, 8.

11. Ibid.

12. Ibid.

13. Ibid.

14. Corrie ten Boom, with John and Elizabeth Sherrill, *The Hiding Place* (Uhrichsville, OH: Barbour and Company, Inc., 1971), 215.

15. "I'm Still Learning to Forgive" by Corrie ten Boom is reproduced with permission from *Guideposts*, Guideposts.org. Copyright © 1972 by Guideposts. All rights reserved.

16. Ibid.

17. *The Hiding Place*, 215.

18. Ibid.

19. "I'm Still Learning to Forgive."

20. *The Hiding Place*, 215.

21. Ibid.

22. "I'm Still Learning to Forgive."

23. "A Service of Word and Table I," *The United Methodist Hymnal,* 8.

24. Ibid.

25. Ibid., 9.

26. Ibid.

27. Jeanne Theoharis, T*he Rebellious Life of Mrs. Rosa Parks* (Boston: Beacon Press, 2013), vii.

28. "A Service of Word and Table I," *The United Methodist Hymnal,* 9.

29. Charles Welsey makes a similar point about the work of the Holy Spirit—the Spirit of Christ—in a hymn for before reading the Scriptures: "unlock the truth, thyself the key, unseal the sacred book" (*The United Methodist Hymnal,* 603).

30. "A Service of Word and Table I," *The United Methodist Hymnal,* 9–10.

31. Ibid., 10.

32. Ibid.

33. In his book *Mere Christianity,* Lewis explores the common ground on which all Christians stand together. He uses the term *mere* not in the sense of meager or inadequate, but rather as an entry point into the fundamental teachings of historic Christianity.

34. Ronald Brown, editor, *Bishop's Brew: An Anthology of Clerical Humour* (New York: Morehouse Publishing, 1990), quoted by Nicky Gumbel, *Questions of Life* (Deerfield, IL: Alpha North America, 2007), 12.

35. "A Service of Word and Table I," *The United Methodist Hymnal,* 10.

36. Ibid.

37. Ibid., 11.

38. Ibid.

39. Ibid.

40. Ibid.

41. See the appendix of this book for the order of worship that we use for the Wednesday service of prayer and Communion. This order can be used as is or adapted as church leaders see fit, and I share it in the hope that it will be a helpful resource for other congregations.

42. *The Great Duty of Frequenting the Christian Sacrifice* was published in 1707 by Robert Nelson. In 1732, Wesley wrote an extract of that treatise for use among Methodists. The shift of emphasis from Nelson's "frequenting the Christian sacrifice" to Wesley's "constant communion" was likely suggested by another tract also read by the early Methodists, *The Constant Communicant* (1681) by Arthur Bury. Wesley wrote his sermon "The Duty of Constant Communion" as an abridgement and revision of his 1732 extract of Nelson's text. When he published the sermon in 1787, Wesley noted that he had not yet "seen cause to alter my sentiments in any point" in that discourse—which shows a strong consistency over time in his views on the importance of the Lord's Supper in the Christian life. The fact that such a low view of its significance is common among Wesley's heirs today is both unfortunate and ironic.

2. Remembering Christ's Presence with Us

1. Pat Summitt with Sally Jenkins, *Sum It Up: 1,098 Victories, a Couple of Irrelevant Losses, and a Life in Perspective* (New York: Crown Archetype, 2013), 376.

2. Ibid.

3. Aaron Kaufman, "The Ugly Truth behind the Super Bowl and Sex Trafficking," *Elite Daily.com* (January 29, 2014), accessed March 4, 2014, http://elitedaily.com/news/world/the-ugly-truth-behind-the-super-bowl-and-sex-trafficking/.

4. After the words of institution, the pastor says: "And so, in remembrance of these your mighty acts in Jesus Christ, we offer ourselves in praise and thanksgiving as a holy and living sacrifice, in union with Christ's offering for us, as we proclaim the mystery of faith" ("A Service of Word and Table I," *The United Methodist Hymnal*, 10).

5. Julian Miglierini, "El Salvador Marks Archbishop Oscar Romero's Murder," *BBC News* (March 24, 2010), accessed March 18, 2014, http://news.bbc.co.uk/2/hi/8580840.stm.

6. "The Duty of Constant Communion," I.2-3, in Wesley, *Works*, 3:429.

7. "The Duty of Constant Communion," I.3, in Wesley, *Works*, 3:429.

8. For example, see *John Wesley's Prayer Book: The Sunday Service of the Methodists in North America*, with introduction, notes, and commentary by James F. White (Cleveland: OSL Publications, 1991).

9. Augustine, *Confessions*, I.1.

10. "A Service of Word and Table I," *The United Methodist Hymnal*, 10.

3. Celebrating the Bread of Life Given for All

1. Thomas Aquinas, *Summa theologiae*, q. 75, a. 1.

2. "O the Depth of Love Divine," *The United Methodist Hymnal*, 627. The hymn as listed above represents a slightly altered version of the original, which reads "God into man" in stanza four (though "man" is meant there in an inclusive sense, as was common in that era). The hymn was first published in John and Charles Wesley, *Hymns on the Lord's Supper* (Bristol: Felix Farley, 1745), an excellent though largely underappreciated resource. A facsimile reprint of the first edition has been published by The Charles Wesley Society (*Hymns on the Lord's Supper* by John Wesley and Charles Wesley with Introduction by Geoffrey Wainwright [Madison, NJ: The Charles Wesley Society, 1995]). Also useful is J. Ernest Rattenbury, *The Eucharistic Hymns of John and Charles Wesley* (London: Epworth Press, 1948); reprint edition, edited by Timothy J. Crouch (Cleveland: Order of St. Luke Publications, 1990).

3. Harry Wiggett, "He Shone with the Light of Christ," *The Church Times* (December 13, 2013), accessed January 17, 2014, http://www.churchtimes.co.uk/articles/2013/13-december/news/world/%E2%80%98he-shone-with-the-light-of-christ%E2%80%99.

4. Ibid.

5. Ibid.

6. For more see David N. Field, "Remembering Madiba—Communing with Christ: Nelson Mandela and the Praxis of Open Communion," *United Methodist Insight* (January 9, 2014), accessed January 17, 2014, http://um-insight.net/perspectives/remembering-madiba-%E2%80%93-communing-with-christ%3A/.

7. *Journal*, June 27, 1740, in *Works*, 19:158. As Wesley wrote in another entry from just five days earlier, "there are *degrees in faith*, and *weak faith* may yet be *true faith*" (*Journal*, June 22, 1740, in ibid., 19:155). Wesley held to the traditional understanding of the Lord's Supper as a meal of the baptized, which therefore assumes at least some degree of faith in Christ on the part of those who receive the Eucharist.

8. *The United Methodist Hymnal*, 7.

9. Brian Wren, "I Come with Joy," *The United Methodist Hymnal*, 617.

4. A Foretaste of the Heavenly Banquet

1. The Wesleys categorically rule out a view of bare memorialism, and nothing more, in phrases like "And eat thy flesh and drink thy blood" and "To every faithful Soul appear, / And show thy Real Presence here" (*Hymns on the Lord's Supper*, hymn 3, stanza 4, line 5; hymn 116, stanza 5, lines 5-6). An inordinate emphasis on the past dimension of the Eucharist tends toward bare memorialism, which in its strict sense reduces the sacrament to an exercise in human memory and thus robs it of (or at best severely limits) its divinely instituted power both as a means of grace in the present and as a pledge of future glory. Positively, the Wesleys had no trouble affirming the Lord's Supper as a memorial insofar as it represents Christ's sufferings and death. The challenge in every age, as described above, is taking a balanced approach that incorporates past, present, and future dimensions appropriately.

2. The significance of Holy Communion for early Methodists finds vivid expression in the Wesleys' *Hymns on the Lord's Supper*. This collection contains spiritually and lyrically rich material that is appropriate not only for worship and teaching in the local church but also for devotional purposes.

3. John Wesley likened faith to a sort of sixth sense in his notion of the spiritual senses, which are senses that God gives us so that we can sense spiritual realities. For example, in *An Earnest Appeal to Men of Reason and Religion*, Wesley describes the spiritual senses by way of analogy to the physical senses:

It is necessary that you have *the hearing ear*, and the *seeing eye*, emphatically so called; that you have a new class of senses opened in your soul, not depending on organs of flesh and blood, to be "the evidence of things not seen" [Hebrews 11:1] as your bodily senses are of visible things; to be the avenues to the invisible world, to discern spiritual objects, and to furnish you with ideas of what the outward "eye hath not seen, neither the ear heard" [1 Corinthians 2:9, Isaiah 64:4]. (*An Earnest Appeal to Men of Reason and Religion*, §32, in Wesley, *Works*, 11:56-57)

4. Charles Wesley, "Come, Thou Long-Expected Jesus," *The United Methodist Hymnal*, 196.

22128127R00069

Made in the USA
Middletown, DE
20 July 2015